WHAT PEOPLE ARE SAYING ABOUT

OF COURSE!

Ian Patrick is a mainstay in   nity –
someone whose dedication   ound
effect on many of us. He h   about Course principles
based on his own life experiences, with reflections that can help
all of us understand and apply them more deeply.
Marianne Williamson, best-selling author of *A Return to Love*,
Illuminata, and *The Age of Miracles*

Ian Patrick has put together a wonderful book that incorporates
many of his articles from *Miracle Worker* magazine. I have read
Ian's work for many years. This book is an important contri-
bution that should be read by any serious student of *A Course in
Miracles*. Be prepared for a quantum leap in your knowledge of
the Course.
Gary Renard, best-selling author of *The Disappearance of the
Universe* and *Your Immortal Reality*

Ian Patrick is 'Mr Miracles'. He is a great ambassador for *A
Course in Miracles*. This wonderful book is testament to his work.
Thank you, Ian, for being an inspiration to me and so many
others.
Robert Holden, PhD, author of *Shift Happens!*

I appreciated Ian's work so much that I urged him to write this
book! And what a wealth of insight he shares with us through
these pages. This is a timely and valuable book; one that reveals
the very 'heart' of all healing – *forgiveness*.
Nouk Sanchez, co-author of *Take Me to Truth: Undoing the Ego*

Think of this book as more of a friendly companion along your spiritual path than yet another 'how to' book. Ian Patrick is able to speak to the part of us that knows Truth, remembers Love, and seeks union. In short, this book is not just a journey through *A Course in Miracles*, it is a gentle voice – sometimes serious and sometimes humorous – awakening something ancient and longed for within each of us. I know Ian Patrick, personally, and I can say he is a man who is always intending to walk what he talks, often taking unique leaps of faith that others only talk about but never do.

Dr Lee Jampolsky, author of *Walking Through Walls* and *Healing the Addictive Personality*

Ian Patrick has written a book with a great deal of love and warmth. We love his informality and good humour. This is, essentially, a personal book. It is as if the reader is meeting a real person. Ian avoids lecturing and is not afraid of connecting at a peer level. He presents a series of brief topics that don't have to be read in order. Those who know nothing about *A Course in Miracles* are not excluded either. Ian knows how to write.

Gerald G. Jampolsky, MD, co-author of *A Mini Course for Life*

"By their fruit you shall know them"… I think this is one of the most powerful spiritual principles around. Many can talk the talk, but when you actually walk the walk you become a miracle worker. It doesn't mean you're perfect (yet), but it does mean that you are willing to walk with God through this world and leave it just a little better. This is how I see Ian Patrick – a dedicated man, who through his book is sharing his 'fruits' with us… helping us to see the miraculous results of walking the walk with God.

Beverly Hutchinson McNeff, co-founder and president of Miracle Distribution Center

Ian Patrick's thoughtful commentaries on the major principles of *A Course in Miracles* are concise, relevant and practical. With courage and sensitivity, he has used his own issues and challenges to illustrate strategic points and to bring the Course's teaching into everyday experience where it belongs. Both beginners and seasoned students will appreciate this most helpful guide.

Carol M. Howe, author of *Never Forget To Laugh: Personal Recollections of Bill Thetford, Co-Scribe of A Course in Miracles*

I am impressed by your splendid and consistent contribution to the spread of the truths in *A Course in Miracles*. It takes a rare combination of dedication, guts and humility to write cogent and persuasive material to a high standard. And it has been heart-warming to see how you have charted some of your own development at the same time, as teacher and loving human being. Thank you and many congratulations on a magnificent achievement and example.

Ken Bradley, ACIM student, Interfaith Minister, 12-Steps sponsor

Ian's articles, which form the basis of the book, are startling in their honesty. He shares how he applies ACIM, albeit imperfectly at times, to the trials of life. We can all relate. His words reach us where we are and move us forward.

Katherine Owen, *www.a-spiritual-journey-of-healing.com*

Of Course!

How Many Light Bulbs
Does It Take to Change

Of Course!

How Many Light Bulbs
Does It Take to Change

Ian Patrick

BOOKS

Winchester, UK
Washington, USA

First published by Fearless Books, 2012
This edition published by O-Books, 2014
O-Books is an imprint of John Hunt Publishing Ltd., Laurel House, Station Approach,
Alresford, Hants, SO24 9JH, UK
office1@jhpbooks.net
www.johnhuntpublishing.com

For distributor details and how to order please visit the 'Ordering' section on our website.

Text copyright: Ian Patrick 2012

ISBN: 978 1 78279 717 3

A CIP catalogue record for this book is available from the British Library.

Design: Stuart Davies

Cover photograph: Kamlan Munsamy

Printed in the USA by Edwards Brothers Malloy

We operate a distinctive and ethical publishing philosophy in all
areas of our business, from our global network of authors to
production and worldwide distribution.

CONTENTS

Foreword

A Course in Miracles is, to me, quite simply the most sophisticated, profound and practical spiritual document ever to surface on planet Earth. It is truly a document of the 20th and 21st centuries. Published in 1976, it has become a modern spiritual classic. Read just a little of the Course and you'll say: "Who wrote this?" This is not coming from someone's ego. There is no axe to grind and it's not trying to sell us anything; rather it is *giving* us the opportunity to experience our own greatest happiness. What the Course says is not new. How could the truth be new? Truth is always true. What is new about the Course is its extremely high level of sophistication. It comes out of perfection. How simple is the truth.

Every now and then, someone will pick up the Course and be so moved by it they feel as though they have 'come home' to the Course and they know that they will be spending the rest of their life studying, living by and teaching this material. That's what happened to my friend, Ian Patrick. Ian had developed a successful career working for major oil companies, and yet something was missing.

Very often, when someone achieves what they are looking for in the external world, they will turn and begin to look within for yet deeper answers. St Francis of Assisi and the Buddha both stepped away from 'worldly success', when they realised that there had to be something more to life than earning money and 'having fun in the world'. Having achieved worldly success and having fun is not enough. If you have achieved worldly success, if the basics are covered, then deeper needs arise – then, often, we start asking more profound questions.

What are we doing here in the first place? How did we get here? Where did we come from? More and more, Ian came to feel that there must be a deeper answer, and "there must be a better way." He began the quest, talking to friends, attending workshops, reading more, listening to lectures and CDs and, lo and behold – those who seek find! He discovered the writings and CDs of our mutual friend, Marianne Williamson. If you've found Marianne, you've also found *A Course in Miracles*.

Although put off at first by the Christian language of the Course, the more Ian studied the Course the more revelatory 'light bulb' moments began to happen for him. At last, he had found his path. He not only began to understand the Course, he began to understand the Christian message in a wholly new light. Ian stopped beating up on himself, and he began to forgive himself in the realisation that "the past as well held no mistakes." (Manual, p. 15) Forgiving himself for what never happened and beginning to give up on guilt, Ian began to enjoy life on a deeper level. Life began to take on purpose. He began to see that, indeed, there was a 'bigger plan'.

We learn best what we teach and so it was that Ian desired to share his joy and what he was learning from the Course. He began a Course study group in his flat. He began *Miracle Worker* magazine. He began the sponsorship of Course workshops with teachers from around the world. He wasn't making as much money as before, but this work was much more evocative and meaningful, and he was having more fun.

As you'll discover in reading *Of Course!*, while Ian has clearly set his foot on the path that leads us all home, he makes no claim on enlightenment or to be a master of the Course. He is, however, clearly someone who has dedicated his life to understanding the Course, and to living the Course as best he can and sharing the Course with as many people as he can. In many ways, Ian is 'Mr Course in Miracles' of the UK. The Miracle Network, which he founded, is now the hub around which many conferences and other ACIM-related events occur in Great Britain.

Ian is a good writer: simple, honest and straightforward. He is easy to read and he often writes in a relaxed conversational style.

You'll also discover, in reading sections like 'The Truth Hurts', that Ian can be funny. He makes no claim at being a scholar, but simply someone who has made a commitment to understanding and applying the principle of *A Course in Miracles* in his own life. What could be better than that?

Jon Mundy, PhD
Author of *Living A Course in Miracles*
Publisher of *Miracles* magazine,
http://www.miraclesmagazine.org

Preface

This book is not intended to be an introduction to *A Course in Miracles* (ACIM). It presupposes some prior knowledge of the principles of the Course and, ideally, some practice at living them. I'm writing primarily for those students of the Course who have been working with the ideas for some time and may have somewhat lost their way or have difficulty in 'seeing the wood for the trees' after sampling the multitude of teachers out there, all with slightly different takes on the Course. Maybe this book is simply *my* take, but I hope it will refocus students who can use a refresher on the essentials. It is like the advanced driving test that people take because they realise that, since passing the initial test long ago, they've picked up all kinds of bad habits along the way that they need to unlearn. Hopefully, this book will assist in some unlearning and refocusing.

In this book, quotations in italics, followed by a page reference, are from the Standard Edition of *A Course in Miracles*, published by the Foundation for Inner Peace, PO Box 598, Mill Valley, CA 94942, a not-for-profit organisation. The words 'Text', 'Workbook' and 'Manual' refer to the three volumes of the Course (bound in one book).

The book you are reading is a selection of essays, written over the course of seventeen years (okay, I'm a slow writer) for the bimonthly *Miracle Worker* magazine, published by the Miracle Network, a UK registered charity. The articles have been arranged in a random order, with the exception of the first four and the last.

I can assure readers that being the author of this book does not mean that I have all the answers. Certainly, of myself alone, I have none. I am not in the position of editor of *Miracle Worker* magazine because my life is one of never-ending joy and happiness, and I would scarcely be human if it were. But I believe

I have a pretty good grasp of the principles of *A Course in Miracles*. I may not always apply them, but I know that, when I apply them, they work.

At times, life has not been easy for me. There have been times when I have felt that I have no business being involved in teaching spiritual principles at all, and that I have made little, if any, progress on my spiritual path.

Is it not like that when you hit a low patch in your life? It's like being in a deep valley in the mountains. The path ahead is not visible; the goal is out of sight; you cannot even see where you have come from, or the spiritual mountains you have already climbed. All that is hidden by the walls of the damn valley you are in! Others tell me how far they see that I have come, when I cannot see it for myself. Likewise, I can see how far they have come when they are at a low point, and have forgotten it themselves.

Sometimes, I am very much concentrated on the world, on earning a living and running the Miracle Network. Sometimes I tell myself that I am so busy I have no *time* to be spiritual. I am so busy rushing about that I forget to ask for help, both internally and externally – or if I do remember, I tell myself that there is no time to meditate or pray.

A Course in Miracles tells us that we have made up the world as a defence against God: a distraction, keeping us preoccupied with externals, to prevent us from looking to the truth within. I can see that the world I have made for myself is pretty good at doing this. After all, I have good reasons for concentrating on it: There's always work to do, including the writing of this book.

There is no doubt that sometimes life is difficult. We may intellectually understand at least some of the principles of *A Course in Miracles*, and we may be sure that the principles work. But when it comes to the crunch, do we *apply* them? It's all too easy to become distracted by the busy sideshows of life: "Yes, I know I haven't done my lesson today, but such and such needs attending to, so I don't have time." So there comes a time when we have to decide between going the spiritual route, or going with worldly distraction. Can we put our money where our mouth is? Do we really believe this stuff?

The whole point of being on a spiritual path is not that we learn to make our way in the world more productively, but that we remember who we *are*. It is difficult enough remembering spiritual principles when we are busy in the world. But beyond that, *applying* the principles instead of just talking about them is the challenge.

The real distraction is the fear that comes with the prospect of letting go. We know there is an answer and that we are not alone on the path. We know there is another way to live than dealing with one distraction after another. The only question left is: Do we have the courage and faith to take the next step, to trust?

The presence of fear is a sure sign that you are trusting in your own strength.

(Workbook, p. 77)

Once Upon A Miracle

Once upon a time, before I came across *A Course in Miracles*, my life was very different from what it is now. Twenty-odd years ago, I was working in the oil industry. I was earning lots of money, more than I could possibly spend. At the age of twenty-five, I had bought a property in central London. I had a car. I travelled the world and had a full social life – a life of seemingly endless parties, drinks after work, relationships (well, more one-night stands than relationships, if I am truly honest). My life was full, yet it felt empty. Something was missing and I didn't know what it was. Even more than my life feeling empty, it was myself who felt empty – empty, alone and purposeless.

One day, I was walking through St James's Park in London with a colleague, Dan, talking about the meaninglessness of life and how I felt like a hamster going endlessly round in its wheel. "What do we do all this for?" I asked. "There must be something more to life than this."

I like to think, if I'm not being grandiose, that it was rather like Bill Thetford's plea to Helen Schucman that "There must be a better way", the result of which was Helen channelling *A Course in Miracles*.

Dan turned to me and told me about someone in the office who had done a course that had really helped him. Dan knew no details, but I immediately decided that I wanted to do this course, even though I had no idea what it was.

The course turned out to be a very powerful EST-type seminar. I learned there, for the first time, that I was responsible for what happens in my life and for my experience of it, whereas before I believed that life just happened to me and I was merely the helpless victim of circumstance. But my biggest gift was meeting people there who led me to psychologist and seminar leader Chuck Spezzano and my first exposure to *A Course in*

Miracles.

> *Tolerance for pain may be high, but it is not without limit. Eventually everyone begins to recognize, however dimly, that there must be a better way. As this recognition becomes more firmly established, it becomes a turning point. This ultimately reawakens spiritual vision, simultaneously weakening the investment in physical sight.*
> (Text, p. 22)

My initial resistance to the Course was largely due to its Christian language. Once I discovered that these 'objectionable' words were being used in profound psychological ways, the Course then felt like coming home. The truths I found in it were what I had been looking for even though I was not even conscious of my search.

"The Forgotten Song" (Text, p. 445) that the Course speaks about is not entirely forgotten and, in fact, plays always in our minds and hearts. Once we recognise it and our dim memory of Home begins to grow, we can never quite be the same. We do all reach our turning point and hear that song, eventually. There are no exceptions.

> *The acceptance of the Atonement by everyone is only a matter of time…You can temporize and you are capable of enormous procrastination, but you cannot depart entirely from your Creator, Who set the limits on your ability to miscreate. An imprisoned will engenders a situation which, in the extreme, becomes altogether intolerable.*
> (Text, p. 21)

My life has meaning and purpose now. It may not look any different on the outside. I still do much the same things as before. I still face challenges and, sometimes, struggles. When I choose to apply the Course's teachings, however, I experience deep peace, joy, and love that are not dependent on circumstances. I know the value of forgiveness and recognise it as my way of healing. I know I am going Home, because I am already there.

Whereas I was blind, now I see.
– John IX, v. 25

The Two Worlds

Picture two worlds, having absolutely nothing in common: the realm of spirit and the material world.

The realm of pure spirit is almost impossible to imagine from here, in the physical world. It is the realm of God, and is referred to as Heaven, our true home. Actually, it's a place we have never left, nor could ever leave in making up this dream world of ours.

In Heaven, there is no separation, only Oneness. No you and me, us and them, good or bad, right or wrong, up or down, then and now. There is only Spirit, *being*. All that exists, exists there in eternal, infinite, formless and never-changing joy, bliss, love, wholeness and perfection. There is no lack or pain, no loss, aloneness, error or imperfection.

There is nothing else besides spirit, and nothing outside or beyond. It is impossible that anything could be beyond or apart from the All. What is a part of that whole always will be so. That will never change.

Beyond the body, beyond the sun and stars, past everything you see and yet somehow familiar, is an arc of golden light that stretches as you look into a great and shining circle. The light expands and covers everything, extending to infinity forever shining and with no break or limit anywhere... Within it everything is joined in perfect continuity. Nor is it possible to imagine that anything could be outside, for there is nowhere that this light is not. (Text, p. 447)

The physical world of time and space, where we experience ourselves as being, is so unlike the realm of spirit as to be unrecognisable if we were able to be 'there' looking at it. This is a world of pain and struggle, suffering and death. Here we spend our lives compensating and making the best of a bad situation. We experience doubt, loss, failure and defeat, but try not to let it get us down. We feel alone and separate, sometimes within long-term relationships. Yet we seek for special relationships of all kinds to make us feel complete, to fill the hole inside, to make up for what we believe is missing.

We fight and attack, blaming others or the world for what we think has been done to us, or for the poor hand we were dealt in life's poker game. We have moments of joy and of love that we fear will not last. And, sure enough and all too soon, these fade away. The best we can do is to hope and pray that tomorrow will be better than today.

Heaven remains your one alternative to this strange world you made and all its ways; its shifting patterns and uncertain goals, its painful pleasures and its tragic joys. God made no contradictions... He did not make two minds, with Heaven as the glad effect of one, and earth the other's sorry outcome which is Heaven's opposite in every way. (Workbook, p. 240)

What we have forgotten, in our deluded minds, is that this world is impossible. It is just not true; in fact, it is a bad dream we are having. But we are being called to awaken to our true Home in Spirit. Like a parent, attempting to awaken a child from a nightmare, the Holy Spirit is calling to us in our dream to awaken to our true Home – in Heaven.

One form of this call to awaken is provided by *A Course in Miracles*. I believe the Course came into the world of illusion from the place of Truth because there was sufficient readiness to listen, despite considerable resistance: our own desire to remain asleep. The Course is a physical manifestation of the Truth, in the form of a book that we can recognise and study. It *had* to come, at some point, and awakening *must* occur, because this world was never true in the first place. Ultimately, it must disappear into the nothingness from whence it came. And the Course is a means for that disappearance.

The world will end in joy, because it is a place of sorrow. When joy has come, the purpose of the world has gone. The world will end in peace, because it is a place of war. When peace has come, what is the purpose of the world? The world will end in laughter, because it is a place of tears. Where there is laughter, who can longer weep?

And only complete forgiveness brings all this to bless the world. In blessing it departs, for it will not end as it began.

(Manual for Teachers, p. 37)

The World is Mad

I just had to laugh when I saw the news one day: **Nelson Mandela meets the Spice Girls!** I ask you, what meaning could there be in such a world? Am I supposed to have any confidence in this kind of reality? And I'm not even talking about considerably more serious craziness like the violence in Bosnia, Afghanistan, Northern Ireland, or Beavis and Butt-head. We look for meaning in a crazy world. Obviously, there is no hope out there.

What is it, then, that attracts me to *A Course in Miracles*? What ensures that I persevere with this discipline despite my resistance, despite the periods when I'm tempted to give up and declare that it does not work? I know that such challenges occur because there is a part of me that wants to use the Course to get a better life, to improve my temporal existence. Don't we all, if we are really honest? In fact, that is probably the initial draw of the Course for everybody. But wanting to use the Course as a coping device for a crazy world, or as a means of enhancing my everyday life, only means I'm trying to improve the illusion.

Even if this is the initial attraction – and that may be by design – I know that is not the Course's ultimate purpose. It means to lead us *beyond* the dream, or at least to a point where we can awaken from it. The Course's purpose is definitely not about making our life better, making our world better, becoming happier or more content with our lives, though those things may well happen along the way. Such developments can be useful devices for our awakening, but it is the awakening itself that the Course points us toward.

What keeps me going with *A Course in Miracles* is the knowledge that it contains Truth. When I read it, I have an experience of Truth that defies rational explanation or analysis; and I know that there is nothing more that I want. Ultimately,

Truth is all there is and all there *can* be. If we were to read the Course merely as an intellectual exercise it would be worthless, but I have always had an *experience* along with that, a form of knowing that goes beyond intellect. The intellectual understanding has to come first, but it is *knowing* that keeps me going even when I resist and resent the Course.

A Course in Miracles transports me to another place entirely. It cuts, razor-like, through the craziness of the world and the craziness of my ego. It does so with such devastating accuracy and blinding clarity that I am left only to laugh at the world's madness and to let it go, momentarily leaving a space for Truth to show itself. I feel at home again.

When I first found the Course, I felt a resonance there, a homecoming. Something inside me said: *Of course, I knew that!* A distant, timeless knowing was revitalized, rekindling a light in me that had been long overlooked but not extinguished. There is nothing more important than seeing that light again.

Listen – perhaps you catch a hint of an ancient state not quite forgotten; dim, perhaps, and yet not altogether unfamiliar, like a song whose name is long forgotten, and the circumstances in which you heard completely unremembered.
(Text, p. 446)

An Upside Down World

The message of *A Course in Miracles* is a radical one – more radical than many of us are able to accept. It is a message that is diametrically opposed to the thinking of the world.

We have all been brought up to think in the way the world does. These upside-down ideas are so deeply ingrained in our minds as to seem instinctive. When we begin the Course, a major challenge is that we get little or no support from the world for pursuing a radical path. It is tempting to take on board only the concepts from the Course that we can readily accept, while glossing over the more radical ideas that we may actively resist. If we are to be legitimate students of the Course, however, we must endeavour to embrace all of the concepts, without editing.

How does the world regard concepts such as its own illusory nature? Or how about *"I am not a body"* (Workbook, p. 382)? How do *you* regard such concepts?

In this world, we are taught that some things are good and others bad; some things are desirable and others not; some things are to be encouraged and embraced, and others resisted. We come to believe that natural things are good, artificial ones bad; that education is good, ignorance bad; that democracy is good, totalitarianism bad; that beauty is good, ugliness bad, and so on.

The radical message of the Course is that the world has *no* inherent value. It is not "good", but the good news is that it's not "bad" either. The world is simply neutral. Any value or meaning that the world, or anything in it, seems to have for us is what we have given to it. It is all in our heads. The world is like a blank canvas on to which we have painted all meaning.

If the world is not to be valued either positively or negatively, then what is it for? *A Course in Miracles* says that the only purpose of the world is that it provides a classroom in which we can learn what Truth is. To find love or achieve happiness has no purpose beyond reminding us of the Truth that lies behind all that we see, feel and experience.

What is that Truth? We think that we are bodies; many of us accept that there is also a part of us that is spiritual. But in fact we are only spirit, pure spirit, and nothing else. This spirit exists in the Oneness of God, eternally. We are not bodies at all. This is all a dream, a hallucination and, for many of us, a nightmare. In the world as we normally experience it, there is no Truth at all.

The self you made is not the Son of God. Therefore, this self does not exist at all. And anything it seems to do and think means nothing. It is neither bad nor good. It is unreal, and nothing more than that. (Workbook, p. 161)

We seem to be here, in the world, only because we *believe* in the reality of the world and that we have separated from God. The only purpose that our daily dream has is to provide opportunities for awakening. Our ego, the part of our mind that believes in the truth of the separation, will never accept these ideas; and so neither will the world.

The message of the Course is that there is also a "decision maker" within our minds who can choose how to use the world. We can choose to remain fearful victims who seem to be at the mercy of circumstances. Or we can use the world to forgive everyone in it, including ourselves, and thus remember who we truly are, and where we are in Reality.

This means that our problems are *never* external, out there in the world; they are *always* in our minds. *"Therefore seek not to change the world, but choose to change your mind about the world."* (Text, p. 445) The Course is not about behaviour modification; it is about a radically different way of thinking. It is simple, but not easy. It is not easy only because we are resistant.

We have within us the ability to decide either in favour of the ego's world of separation, guilt and fear; or to ask the Holy Spirit, the force in our minds that can transform perception, to guide our thinking so that forgiveness returns us to the Reality of our Being, the Truth of Heaven.

Forgiveness gently looks upon all things unknown in Heaven, sees them disappear, and leaves the world a clean and unmarked slate on which the Word of God can now replace the senseless symbols written there before... Forgiveness lets the body be perceived as what it is; a simple teaching aid, to be laid by when learning is complete, but hardly changing him who learns at all.
(Workbook, p. 365)

In every difficulty, all distress, and each perplexity Christ calls to you and gently says, "My brother, choose again."
(Text, p. 666)

The Quickening

We live in interesting times. I've sensed a quickening or "celestial speedup" (to borrow Jesus' phrase given to Helen Schucman) in my own life. And world events seem to have reflected this.

Few happenings on the world stage have had more impact on us, both as individuals and nations, than those of 11th September 2001. In the immediate aftermath, I found myself wanting to react impulsively. But I held off. I wanted the dust to settle, in more ways than one, to get a clearer perspective. This section is my attempt to address, in a measured way, what such events in the world mean to us and how the Course teaches us to respond.

Faced with any situation, but particularly a tragedy on the scale of 9/11 and what followed, we have two options: fear or love.

Usually we take the first option: fear. I lost track of the number of urgent emails I received, following the 9/11 attacks and the launch of the war in Afghanistan, calling for emergency prayers to fix the world situation. Of course, the urge to attack back, militarily, is also coming from fear. It is so tempting for all of us to go down the fear route. It is the first reaction. And, in the face of feelings of fear, there is another attractive position: denial. "What attacks? What war? *A Course in Miracles* says that the world is an illusion. Right? So there is no war, really."

So what approach can students of the Course take? The one true alternative is love: healing, acceptance and forgiveness of what we see, without denial. In other words, we need to ask first what our fear, shock, grief, sadness and anger tell us about ourselves. How can we truly join with our brothers in healing our misperceptions and our wounds, in remembering the truth and finding peace? These are the lessons of the Course.

There is no such thing as world peace, only collective inner peace. Certainly, if the perpetrators of any attack had been feeling inner peace and had felt connected to their inherent wholeness, there would have been no attack. So we must begin at home. When I perceive attack, even such a monumental one as 9/11, it triggers guilt about my own capacity for attack, albeit in lesser form. When I see murder and abuse, I am shocked because I know that I too am capable of thoughts of murder and abuse.

I find that situations like these are opportunities for forgiveness, to truly join with my brothers (without condoning behaviour). World crises are opportunities to either stay asleep and fearful, or open my heart and mind to other possibilities. By doing this, I experience the true innocence of others and myself and thus take a giant step towards my personal salvation and thence the salvation of the world.

Light in the Tunnel

Someone asked me about the pain, fear, depression and negativity she had been experiencing since she started *A Course in Miracles* about fifteen years ago. Many times, she had been tempted to throw the Course in the bin. Her fear had reached such a degree that, when given the opportunity to ask a question at an ACIM workshop, she became so overwhelmed that she could not even speak into the microphone. She asked me about evil spirits and fear; having been treated for depression since beginning the Course, she was wondering when the light would appear in her particular tunnel. This is a dramatic case, but who has not felt like this at times? Kenneth Wapnick went so far as to say that if you have not been tempted to throw the Course away, you are not doing it correctly!

When things appear to be getting worse, instead of resulting in the joy and healing we anticipate, it may be tempting to believe that the Course is not working. It may even seem to be intensifying your chronic problems, or causing you difficulties you did not have previously.

The Course says that we come into the world with our egos dominating our experience, though we are unaware of it. Most people are wearing some kind of mask – happy, cynical, angry, religious, victimised, apathetic, resigned, or what have you – that they believe is the truth of themselves and below which they rarely look. Underneath every kind of mask, the ego is alive and well, keeping the whole system going, happy that this false front is in place and the denial almost complete.

When we commence *A Course in Miracles*, we begin to undo layers of that denial in our minds. We start to see the ego for what it is, with all its devious and unhealthy ways. We look fear in the eye; the unconscious becomes more conscious. And this means that some kind of struggle erupts. But the problematic ego was there long before; we were simply denying it. Suddenly, we can deny it no longer – no matter how hard we may try!

The Course did not create our problems. But it has shone a light upon them, so we now have a clearer sight of what's really going on. It is like putting dirty plates in washing-up water – bits of food waste pop up to the surface and float there. It looks like you have created a mess, but this is actually the beginning of the cleaning process.

As the light comes nearer you will rush to darkness, shrinking from the truth, sometimes retreating to the lesser forms of fear, and sometimes to stark terror. But you will advance, because your goal is the advance from fear to truth.
(Text, p. 378)

So, when our spiritual path gets rocky and new problems appear to arise out of nowhere, it is actually good news. You are not possessed by an evil spirit after all. What seems like bad news is really a cause for celebration. It means that the ego's foundations have been shaken.

That said, so-called depression may be real from a medical or therapeutic perspective, and the pressure of it can be so great that we can benefit from conventional therapy or medication (what the Course calls "magic") to lighten the load a bit and become more receptive to the assistance of spiritual practice. So, if your doctor prescribes antidepressants or someone suggests psychoanalysis, there is nothing wrong with following such professional advice.

The ego's capacity to use anything and everything to delay your awakening cannot be underestimated. The ego will pose as your friend, pretending that it is acting in your best interests when it warns you against your chosen spiritual practice. Beware the egoistic cries of: "It's not working," "It's making things worse," "This is not the course for you" and, especially, "You've failed – again!" and "You're a lost cause." To quote the poet William Blake: "Don't believe the lie."

No Answers Out There

Sometimes the problems of life are so numerous and intractable that they seem impossible to overcome. When we begin to study *A Course in Miracles*, we might expect that it will somehow solve them all! It is true that the Course offers the answer to our problems, but not in the way we thought; they do not just stop happening.

I woke up one morning with my head full of thoughts about all the different areas of my life that were not working. I had money worries, relationship worries, job worries, worries about the future, about my health and about getting old. There is always something in this life, isn't there? Typically, there will be problems with family, parents, partner, children; the boss, noisy neighbours, old what's-his-name who kept doing so-and-so; the house that is too small, too old, in the wrong position; or lack of self-esteem. On this particular morning, I wondered how I could get it all to work. It was too much, and I did not know how to begin dealing with any of it.

Then, I realised that, in truth, there are no answers out there because the problems are not out there. It is so liberating to know that the world was set up by the ego precisely *not* to work; it's meant to represent the opposite of the peace of Heaven. The world was set up by the ego as a smokescreen to deceive and distract us from ever looking at our one and only problem. Putting it simply, we have forgotten who we are.

We made a silly mistake in believing we could be separate from our creator. And, having come to believe that, we have successfully created enough evidence to confirm that belief and to forget that we ever made a mistaken choice. The world is nothing more than a diversion – and a very effective one – which we made so that we could lose our way. Once we believe we are here, we believe our problems and their solutions are here too –

as my morning turmoil so clearly demonstrated. The truth is that the world will never work. It is a dysfunctional place, because the ego that made it is a dysfunctional thought.

The ego wants us to be preoccupied with fruitlessly trying to sort it all out. It loves us to be unhappy. It will rub its hands with glee at our misery, so long as it keeps us looking at the problem where it is not – in the world – and for a solution where there is none. Or it will encourage us to deny our pain and pretend that everything is wonderful in the world. Either way, it wants us never to question that the ego is our friend. It wants us never to look inside our mind to where the true problem – the thought of separation – lies and where our true Friend, the Holy Spirit, lives.

Once we realise that the world will never be problem-free, we will give up trying to fix it and begin to laugh at the craziness of ego-thinking, thus allowing ourselves to reconnect with the sanity that rests within our mind.

As we practise doing this, it becomes easier. It is not that our problems disappear, but they cease to be perceived as problems. They are now seen as opportunities to reconnect with the inner Friend, who always has the solution. Then our life becomes an experience of alternately forgetting and remembering. The measure of our progress is not the absence of problems, but how well we deal with those problems as they occur. As we practise, it simply takes less time for us to remember; this is the "happy dream."

Does the world begin to work as our mind becomes more aligned with spirit? Maybe. As we let go of our guilt and our projections on to the world, our experience can only improve. *But a world that works is no more true than one that does not.* Both distract us into thinking that the action is *out there.*

Nothing in the world will ever work, in the sense of bringing the peace of mind we seek. The way of *A Course in Miracles* is to see the world differently, through the forgiving vision of the Holy Spirit, rather than the condemning eyes of the ego.

Will the world ever work better? Maybe, maybe not. The key understanding on the spiritual path is that it does not matter either way. It is no longer the issue. Eventually we cease to believe in the reality of the drama.

The World's Not Here

Of all the ideas in *A Course in Miracles*, the one that always produces the most resistance, repulsion and indignation, especially amongst new students, is the idea that the world we experience is an illusion or dream, and that God did not create this world. The related concepts that God does not even know about this world, and that the Holy Spirit does not operate within the dream to help us improve it, seem particularly hard for us to accept.

Of course, I know these concepts sound a bit bizarre at first, to say the least. The world does not accept its own falsity; we do not read about it in the newspapers or on TV. Imagine: "**Exclusive: WORLD NOT REAL – Shocking new report from our Metaphysical Correspondent**"! Yet, this is not bad news. It is the best news possible! It means that God did not make all the bad things in the world – the wars, disasters, death, etc. It means that we are not tiny, weak bodies that get ill and die. And it means that God is not insane. If the world was real and God knew about it, then our separation from Him would indeed have happened. It would mean that a part of God's One Love, which is all, could split itself off and become something else. If God knew about the world and believed this could happen, then He would be as insane as we are, and there would truly be no hope.

The world's unreality explains why nothing we try to do or change in the world ever succeeds in the long term – because there is no problem "out there" in the world. Nothing "out there" in the world can bring us what we are looking for. But the good news is that nothing in the world can hurt us either.

If there is no world, the solution to any problem we have is not outside of us, out of reach. It is in our minds, where we can choose again to hear the voice of the Holy Spirit. There is nothing out there to fight against. This is good news.

The reality of this concept makes the acceptance of the Atonement possible. Otherwise, we are stuck here! It is the reason that *"There is no order of difficulty in miracles"* (Text, p. 3) – because one times nothing is no different than one thousand times nothing, or a billion times nothing.

The idea of an illusory world, of which God knows nothing, is the foundation stone on which the principles of *A Course in Miracles* rest. It is very good news indeed.

There is no world! This is the central thought the course attempts to teach. Not everyone is ready to accept it, and each one must go as far as he can let himself be led along the road to truth. He will return and go still farther, or perhaps step back a while and then return again. But healing is the gift of those who are prepared to learn there is no world, and can accept the lesson now. Their readiness will bring the lesson to them in some form which they can understand and recognize. Some see it suddenly on point of death, and rise to teach it. Others find it in experience that is not of this world, which shows them that the world does not exist because what they behold must be the truth, and yet it clearly contradicts the world.
(Workbook, p. 243)

Finally, I think it is a mistake to believe that the beauty of nature or works of art show that the world is good. In truth, the ego is very selective in what it sees. Nature is a good example: tree roots strangle each other and animals compete and kill to survive. The world is not good, but it is not bad either. It is not to be escaped from, or denied. It is simply a mistake – nothing. We can enjoy the world while we appear to be here, without believing in it; without taking it too seriously.

So the world is not wonderful in itself. But if you look at it with your right mind, with the Holy Spirit, then you can have an experience of the world that is wonderful.

What better news could you wish for?

The Good, the Bad, and the Same

I have been studying *A Course in Miracles* intensely for years. For much of that time, I have been aware of two different and contradictory approaches to the Course. For the sake of this article, I will label the two approaches, perhaps unfairly, as the *negative* and the *positive* ways. I have struggled to come to terms with these two schools of thought and somehow reconcile them. I have spent a lot of time trying to decide which way is consistent with the Course. I have even tried denying that there *are* any differences.

The negative approach, most conspicuously taught and encouraged by Kenneth Wapnick, puts the emphasis on looking at the ego, in all its horror. It is the angle which emphasises the ego's lies, its desire to keep us in guilt, its motives of attack and murder, its wish to keep its motives hidden through denial, and finally its need to be right, whatever the consequences.

The positive school of thought teaches that having forgotten who we are as Christ, all we need to do is remember. It teaches that to awaken, we must recognise our innocence, that we are one with our Creator and Source, and that we are, in essence, the presence of love.

The positive approach is taught by the majority of ACIM teachers. It is a message that should not be overlooked or undervalued. I have no doubt that it teaches the truth and that it is an integral part of our path of awakening. But, most times, the positive approach is not the one that really helps me. I believe that the Course wants us to look unflinchingly at the ego and that its author has excellent reasons for placing such a great weight on descriptions of the ego's murderous thought system.

The advantage of taking the negative approach, in my experience, is that when we find ourselves tempted by thoughts of guilt, fear or attack – as we inevitably will – we will see them for what they are. We will know, accept and understand why egos do what they do. We will be able to say: "Here we go again! So what's new?" We will not feel guilty for feeling guilty, which is the double bind the ego desires. Being able to say: "So what's new?" – in other words, being able to laugh gently at the ego – is to look through the forgiving eyes of the Holy Spirit. And it is this that undoes the ego, making space for the memory of God to return.

It seems to me that the risk of the positive way is that, in the heat of the moment, one is likely to respond to inevitable ego thoughts this way: *"Not again! This is not how I am supposed to think."* Then the temptation is to feel guilty for having such ego thoughts. For the ego, any kind of guilt will do and, thus, we end up looking at the ego *with* the ego. The ego always takes itself very seriously and has no hesitation in saying, *"Isn't it awful"* about itself. And that just keeps us stuck in ego thinking.

Like most people, I do not find it easy to catch the ego before it "gets me." Maybe it will become easier with practice. But when I am able to do it, I know that adopting a *"So what's new?"* attitude towards the ego actually undoes it – every time.

Before we are able to remember the truth of Who we are, it is necessary that the ego be undone. It is only then that the Holy Spirit, the ever-present memory of God's love in our minds, is able to show us that we are, indeed, the presence of love. I just don't think there are any shortcuts to this process. I believe that the attempt to jump to the "good" stuff is due to our fear of looking at the "bad" (which we secretly believe is our reality) and thus is simply a form of denial.

The apparent contradictions between the positive and negative approaches have been resolved for me, not by deciding between them or by trying to make them be the same, but by the realisation that they are both required in the awakening process – but sequentially.

Thus, in any painful circumstance, the process is: Look first at the ego with total honesty, and with the Holy Spirit, *then* remember the truth of our reality as the presence of love.

Hierarchy of Illusions

One of the most common pitfalls encountered by students of *A Course in Miracles* is thinking that the Course means less than it actually does. This often manifests as the idea that the Course is a guide to behaviour, a kind of moral code for living in the world.

But the Course is only interested in our *thoughts*, particularly whether we are focusing on the thought of fear or love. It is not interested in our behaviour. It is not interested in what you do or say, *per se*. It is not interested in form, but only in content. Thus, ACIM is not telling us that we are better students if we hug someone, rather than shake their hand. We are not better students if we vote for one particular political party over another, or stay away from politics. It is not about being vegetarian, or environmentally friendly, and so on. What matters is what's driving our behaviour – love or fear?

Once, for reasons I considered to be in my mother's best interests, I withheld some information from her. I struggled to decide what was kindest and that's how I decided to handle it. Unfortunately, the truth slipped out and I had to come clean. When I told a friend what had happened, he responded that by telling the truth, I had "brought illusion to Truth." He said I should write about this in *Miracle Worker* magazine to give readers "permission to step out of their imagined selves and choose something different."

These fine-sounding words actually mask the confusion I am talking about. Somehow, my action of telling the truth was considered better than withholding the information, despite my loving reasons for withholding it. It was also perceived that one action was 'more true' than another and thus more spiritual.

The Course tells us that nothing here is real. Therefore, no action here has any reality or relation to Truth. What matters is:

What is it for? And: *Is my thinking based on love or fear?*

The Course is certainly about bringing illusions to the Truth. It is not about the reverse; that is, bringing metaphysical ideas down to the worldly level to direct our behaviour in the world. Doing this weakens the real message of the Course and serves only to *"make* [the] *error real"* (Text, p. 215) in our minds.

Speaking of the *"laws that rule the world we made"* – that is, what we think is right and wrong in the world – the Course says that these laws derive

> *... from the belief there is a hierarchy of illusions; some are more valuable and therefore true. Each [person] establishes this for himself, and makes it true by his attack on what another values.*
> (Text, p. 489)

We all tend to believe that there is a hierarchy of illusions. For example, we are inclined to see some people as more special, valuable, or lovable than others. This hierarchy leads us into tricky territory, because it establishes an "unreal reality" and makes some miracles seemingly harder than others. The Course corrects this idea in the statement in the 'Principles of Miracles':

> *There is no order of difficulty in miracles. One is not 'harder' or 'bigger' than another. They are all the same. All expressions of love are maximal.*
> (Text, p. 3)

What we are encouraged to do is to bring illusion to the Truth, which means letting our issues, grievances, attachments and disappointments go, forgiving and surrendering them to the Holy Spirit for correction.

> *Bringing illusion to truth, or the ego to God, is the Holy Spirit's only function. Keep not your making from your Father, for hiding it*

has cost you knowledge of Him and of yourself.
(Text, p. 291)

His judgement, then, is that:

Every loving thought is true. Everything else is an appeal for healing and help, regardless of the form it takes.
(Text, p. 215)

Life Doesn't Work If We Don't

I can categorically state that *A Course in Miracles* does not work! What do I mean by this? I mean that although we may study the book to obtain beneficial effects, the Course itself does not do anything *to* us. We can ascribe magic powers to this book if we want, but magic does nothing and does not exist in truth. It is only by practising what the Course teaches that we will awaken to truth. In other words, it is we who do it, *not* the book.

That may seem obvious, but how often do we give magic powers to things outside ourselves – be it pills, crystals, healthy food, money, relationships, new jobs, and so on? We rely on those things to give us something, whether it is health, peace, prosperity, or love.

By doing this we have reversed the principle of cause and effect. We think that the external situation (the apparent cause) will have an effect on our internal well-being. In fact, it is our thoughts that are cause, the effects of which we perceive in the world. Nothing in the so-called outside world can ever do anything (desirable or undesirable) to us because, in truth, there is no outside world to do it.

Have you ever had an experience like this? I woke up one morning in a foul mood – angry, depressed, disillusioned – for no reason that I could put my finger on. The day was terrible. If something could go wrong, it did, from my computer not working to a cheque bouncing. I felt alone and unloved, and went to bed in the same negative frame of mind. Next morning, for no reason that I could put my finger on, the cloud had lifted. I woke feeling happy and contented. None of the circumstances that had weighed me down the previous day had been changed overnight, yet I felt lighter, at peace and happy. The day was a breeze – my computer miraculously worked, I felt truly abundant and the telephone never stopped ringing with all my friends calling for a chat.

Whatever I chose manifested in my world. I had no reason for either choice, I simply chose it. And I know which choice I preferred!

The principle of cause and effect is a fundamental one, both in Heaven and in our everyday world. But we have the concepts reversed in our minds. *The cause is always our thinking; the effect is always our experience.*

It was our collective choice, apparently, to embark on a *"detour into fear"* (Text, p. 17), or the dream of separation. That's the cause of the world we experience. Though we have forgotten, we are always "at cause." And it is our choice whether or not we return our minds to the truth of our inheritance.

> *The separation started with the dream the Father was deprived of His Effects, and powerless to keep them since He was no longer their Creator...* [The body and the world appear] *to prove the dreamer could not be the maker of the dream. Effect and cause are first split off, and then reversed, so that effect becomes a cause; the cause, effect.*
> (Text, p. 594)

We are responsible for our spiritual growth and our awakening. Simply reading *A Course in Miracles* and understanding the principles is not sufficient. We must use its principles to correct the cause. The Holy Spirit is our guide, his light showing us the way, but he will not do the job for us. The only hope for our salvation is that *we* bring the ego's illusions to be corrected by the Holy Spirit's truth in our minds.

> *God's answer lies where the belief in sin must be, for only there can its effects be utterly undone and without cause. Perception's laws must be reversed, because they are reversals of the laws of truth. The laws of truth forever will be true, and cannot be reversed; yet can be*

seen as upside down. And this must be corrected where the illusion of reversal lies.
(Text, p. 554)

Who Are We?

A *Course in Miracles* says that our only problem is that we have forgotten who we are (Workbook, pp. 141–144). This forgetting came about as the result of a decision to take the idea of the separation seriously. But what led up to the separation, and what bearing does that have on our day-to-day lives? Is there a connection between this metaphysical idea and our happiness?

The Course says that the separation came about as a result of the Son of God wanting to be different from His Father, wanting something more than the Everything that was already his; above all, wanting to go his own way and do his own thing, as if he knew better than God what was good for him. That's the theory.

In practice, every time we are unhappy about something, we are saying: "I would be happy if..." We are saying: "If this thing was the way I want, then I'd be happy." What we are really saying is that we know what would make us happy and we'd be happy if things always go our way. This is the thinking of a spoilt child. In fact, a lot of our unhappiness and depression is much like a child stamping his foot and saying: "I want...!" and remaining upset until he gets what he's after. Every time we are unhappy, we are telling God that we know best what is good for us. We are telling Him what we want. We think we need more of this, less of that, to see more of this person, less of that one, and so on. We want to have only good things happen to us and, by and large, we want them all now!

It is quite natural, of course, for our ego minds to work this way, but this mindset is rooted in the original thought of separation. According to the Course, every unhappiness, desire and feeling of lack owes to replaying, reliving and reinforcing the original thought that we can go off and do our own thing.

Has this strategy worked? Is advancement on the spiritual path measured merely by our ability to have life go the way we want? I don't think so. Has getting anything you thought you wanted brought you the lasting happiness you expected it to? No – temporary relief, maybe, but only temporary because getting that thing was not, deep down, what you really craved.

Once we have recognised the error of this strategy and accepted that there is a better way, we can turn any situation over to the Holy Spirit. We can say: "I don't know what is in my best interests. I don't know what this is for. I don't know what any of this means. My upset is due to the meaning I have given to this situation. I don't know what would make me happy. Please show me. Please provide this situation with Your meaning. Please show me what would actually make me happy."

When we do this, we are aligning our mind with the truth, because behind everything we think we want, what we *actually* want is the peace of God. It is only reconnecting with God that can truly make us happy and, somewhere in our minds, we know that to be true.

How Not to be Spiritual

I once gave a presentation to the ACIM Conference in Manchester entitled "How Not to be Spiritual." The point I was making with this facetious title was about recognising and forgiving our human-ness.

So long as we are in a body or, more accurately, *believe* that we are in one, we will have human desires and needs. And they are okay; they are not unspiritual. I believe it's important to accept where we are on the path and to accept that we fall short of being fully realised spiritual beings.

As we know, the ego loves to judge. If we judge ourselves for feeling angry and fearful, for having human needs, making mistakes, or even for having judgements, we end up in a double bind. It is one more turn of the ego's screw when we beat ourselves up.

In another chapter, I write about being on a giant Ferris wheel at a funfair, hurtling round at break-neck speed, and feeling absolutely terrified. My friend, sitting next to me, equally scared, kept shouting: "It's only an illusion!" He was correct, but at the same time, it was okay for me-in-a-body to be terrified. It was more appropriate for me to accept myself than to attempt a metaphysical leap beyond myself. Kenneth Wapnick reminded us often in his teachings to "remember to be normal." Gary Renard says, more colourfully: "Don't be weird." For example, we do not have to pretend that we are not sick when we are, or to feel that we have failed as Course students if we go to the doctor.

I remember once feeling angry about something and trying all the tricks in the miracle book to let it go. I prayed, undertook forgiveness exercises and did a lesson, but still felt angry. Finally, I realised that I just wanted to be angry that day, and that was perfectly all right. I forgave myself for being angry. Immediately, the pressure was off and I even began to enjoy stomping around.

Suffering comes from resisting our pain.

I am not suggesting that we do nothing to heal our minds. At the same time that we accept exactly where we are on the path, it's important to keep an eye on the goal and move in that direction. But *acting* spiritual is *not the goal*. The Course is always aimed at our thinking, not our behaviour.

For example, we do not have to make an effort to act in a certain way in order to be loving and kind. When our thoughts are aligned with the Holy Spirit, we will be automatically loving and kind.

Likewise, thinking that we must deprive ourselves to be spiritual is *not the goal*. *"My meaningless thoughts are showing me a meaningless world"* (Workbook, p. 18) does not mean we do not do things in the world. It just means that they are meaningless. *"I will not value what is valueless"* (Workbook, pp. 245–7) does not mean we have to avoid caring about things. It just means that they are valueless. It is how we think about what we do that counts.

Back to basics: One can have the most outrageously colourful sex life, for example, or choose to have none at all. What does it matter? So long as you are in a body, do whatever floats your boat. What *does* matter is your thinking – the meaning you give to what you do, your attachments, needs, etc. It is the latter that causes suffering and what the ego loves to hold you hostage to.

I have heard people talk about the dark side of humanity. There is no dark side! As Shakespeare wrote in *Hamlet*: "There is nothing either good or bad, but thinking makes it so."

Correcting your thinking – which, with your willingness, is the job of the Holy Spirit – brings the recognition of truth and restores the awareness of your grandeur and wholeness. And it is an entirely *internal* process.

Wealth, Wholeness and Holiness

Do you feel abundant? Even if you do not, I maintain that you *are* truly abundant. As a Creation of God, how could you not be?

I am not talking about abundance on the level of form, in the material world. *A Course in Miracles* is not concerned with that level. Rather, it is urging us to surrender our attachments to the world, so that they may be undone. However, the very function of the material realm is to keep our attention "out there", on the form. If we look out there, we *will* perceive lack because we'll be trapped in the ego's world of finite resources and scarcity.

Since we make our own reality, we can make whatever we want in this world. We can be as abundant or as impoverished as we want. The pitfall is the temptation to look for the external, material trappings of abundance, making them the goal.

Efforts at increasing our material abundance may work (unless there are other unrecognised, unconscious motivations at play), but they are really just tinkering with the illusion, and will tend to keep us focused on the external world. It is not wrong to wish for things, to play with the illusion. Material abundance, be it money or anything else, is not good or bad. Like everything in the world, it is neutral. It is only the *attachment* to those things that causes us pain.

The dreaming of the world takes many forms, because the body seeks in many ways to prove it is autonomous and real. It puts things on itself that it has bought with little metal discs or paper strips the world proclaims as valuable and real. It works to get them, doing senseless things, and tosses them away for senseless things it does not need and does not even want.
(Text, p. 585)

Since form is the effect of our thoughts, our material abundance can be seen as a measure of how abundant we feel. It is a measure of the value you place on yourself – a measure, nothing more.

While we may be distracted by the external world, the real action is taking place internally. Our true abundance lies inwardly – in *who we are* in truth. Our task is not to *become* more abundant; we are already abundant. Our task is to undo our blocks to the awareness of the abundance that is already ours. The preoccupation with form is a major block to that awareness.

According to Course teacher Nick Davis, in his book *The Golden Steps to Prosperity*, the word *wealth* originates from the ancient word *wholth*, meaning wholeness – or in *A Course in Miracles* language, 'holiness'. He writes: "A prosperity consciousness is a mind that believes it has everything it needs." As creations of God, we were created with everything that has real value – love, peace, joy, wholeness. The Son of God can never be in need or lack anything, since these Gifts were given to him forever at his creation. Lao-tzu said: "He is rich who knows he has enough."

The miracle is changing your mind from lack to abundance. It is a recognition of your wholeness. The Holy Spirit will not look after your bank balance, but He will look after your fear about your bank balance.

Abundance is not about having money, possessions or material comfort, although these things will reflect the abundance you feel within. Abundance is Who you are. It is your true, whole nature. You do not have to achieve or earn it. You *are* it. It is the glory and the Love of God, your connectedness with all, within and without. It is the rapture of knowing your Self in a real sense.

Begin a practice of sitting quietly in meditation and reflecting on the Wholeness of God that you are. See if you can learn to feel the incredible joy of that connection, that reality. That is abundance. What more could there possibly be? What are these mere trinkets we value so much in the world compared with the wonder of the All?

Truth is always abundant. Those who perceive and acknowledge that they have everything have no needs of any kind.
(Text, p. 11)

Acceptance and Forgiveness

Several years ago, I spent the best part of a year travelling the length of Africa in a truck with a small group of Australians. It was an incredible, life-changing experience in many ways – not least of which were the many opportunities I was presented with to forgive Australians!

I loved life on the open road, the excitement of new countries and landscapes. Most of all, I loved meeting people from vastly different cultures and backgrounds, realising that we had far more in common than the things that seemed to separate us.

One of the most significant lessons I learned about myself was how easy it was, in those circumstances, for me to let go and move with the flow of events. As on any such expedition, there were many challenges and setbacks to be experienced. Whether it was mechanical breakdowns, illness, physical discomfort, encounters with bribery and corruption, adverse weather conditions or theft (all of which occurred in abundance), I was able to accept everything as being part of the African experience. "This is what happens in Africa," I reasoned to myself, "so it is okay." I had journeyed there for an adventure, and what kind of adventure would it have been if everything had gone smoothly?

What I have found more difficult is to apply this same thinking to my everyday life back home. I don't know why it is so difficult; really there should be no difference. In fact, my African experience is a beautiful analogy for the larger experience of life. *A Course in Miracles* tells us that, as the Son of God, we chose to go our own way, wondering if it was possible to leave our Father to have a little adventure on our own. Challenges and setbacks are an inevitable aspect of this separated dream state, as they were for me on my African adventure. Everything that occurs is part of the life adventure.

Yet, instead of going with the flow and accepting my

everyday experiences as they happen, I have noticed that my expectations and attachments get in the way, destroying my peace of mind and happiness, time after time. My ego is attached to outcomes; it wants things to go its own way. The Holy Spirit, on the contrary, fully accepts all situations, knowing that each one is the perfect classroom for my learning. He is also fully accepting of me and my mistakes.

Attainment of a state of being without attachments is a common theme amongst the world's religions. In Buddhism, it is regarded as the essence of enlightenment. Lao-tzu taught that we should be like a river, flowing effortlessly without struggling or grasping. Religions teach living by faith or, as the Twelve Step saying goes: *Let go and let God.*

The problem with my psychological attachments, whether to people, things or events, is that like physical attachments, they keep me stuck. An attachment or aversion to anything in my mind binds me to the illusion of that thing and thus has the effect of making the illusion seem real.

If I can remain vigilant and hand my attachments over to the Holy Spirit, I will be released from them. As I am released from attachments, I am freed from illusions. As I am, in turn, freed from illusions I am able to remember the truth about myself: that I am a free spirit, at one with my Creator – and not a limited entity, in a physical body, destined to fall prey to all manner of influences from an external and unfriendly world.

I think the aim of a student of *A Course in Miracles* is to learn to tread lightly through life. As Kenneth Wapnick said: "Do whatever you do. Just don't make it a big deal" – take it too seriously.

If this was a natural ability for me in the heart of Africa, it can become a natural ability for me at home, too.

The Blocks to Love's Presence

Have you ever wondered why so much of *A Course in Miracles* is devoted to descriptions of horror? Why is there so much about murder, flesh being ripped from bone, wanting to fling people over cliffs, etc? For example:

> *And both will walk in danger, each intent, in the dark forest of the sightless... to lead the other to a nameless precipice and hurl him over it. For what can specialness delight in but to kill? What does it seek for but the sight of death? Yet is it joy to look upon decay and madness, and believe this crumbling thing, with flesh already loosened from the bone and sightless holes for eyes, is like yourself?*
> (Text, pp. 509–10)

> *And in* [fear's messengers'] *savage search for sin they pounce on any living thing they see, and carry it screaming to their master, to be devoured.*
> (Text, p. 410)

Is all this really necessary? Does Jesus have an unhealthy penchant for such talk? If this is a book about love and peace, why is there so much that describes the opposite of that in graphic detail? Why does Jesus bang on about the ego's desire to attack and murder over hundreds of pages? Why does he do that and then say that none of it is real anyway? If none of it is real, then can't we just forget about it?

In fact, the Course is very clear that it is *not* a book about love. On the very first page it says that love is beyond what can be taught and that it is a book about removing the blocks to the awareness of love's presence. As Michael Dawson says, love does not have to be generated; it simply shines forth when the blocks are removed.

The Course is a book about the blocks. Jesus describes in painful detail the ego's horror and murderous intentions not because he believes they are real, or in any way important – but because *we* do. These are *our* blocks to love. Jesus is merely saying: "Look."

The part of us that does not want to look, that is repulsed by these images of death, is the part of us that believes them to be real and therefore fears and feels guilty about them. It is the part of us that we call the ego. It could only be the ego that is horrified. For the Holy Spirit would see such craziness and laugh.

The Holy Spirit's response to the original "tiny, mad idea" that we could be separate from God is to let us know that it was a foolish and impossible thought. It was the ego that took the idea seriously, believed that it could happen and believed that the consequences would be terrible. So the ego has lived in guilt and fear ever since.

The trick, then, is to continue to look at our blocks, even though we are repulsed. This is a useful insight into our psyche. *Not* looking does not make the blocks go away, it *preserves* them. We are just pretending that they are not there.

The Course's method is to look at the blocks with the Holy Spirit, see them in all their gory terror without judgement and guilt, see the insanity that believes that this could be the Son of God's reality, and then forgive ourselves for such foolishness.

Knowledge to Experience

I have come to realise that it is very easy to pay lip service to the principles of *A Course in Miracles* while really believing something quite different.

How many of us would not jump out of the way of a huge truck bearing down on us as we crossed the road? We *do* believe in the reality of this world, even if we claim that we don't. Let's be honest: nobody I know would calmly face the truck without fear. This is precisely the lesson that Jesus taught – he knew that death is not real – but how many of us could be nailed to a cross and feel no fear? We are simply not yet at Jesus' level. Let's be honest.

It's very easy for us to say that our brothers are innocent, or that death is not real while secretly hiding thoughts of murder and revenge, and fearing for the future. The ego loves to be "spiritual". Using spiritual language and adopting spiritual behaviour does not mean anything. Behind the 'spiritual' mask that we may like to show the world often lies intense rage, attack thoughts and self-hatred. Let's be honest.

This is not a reason to condemn ourselves, though inevitably we will – such is the nature of ego. The message of the Course is simple, but it is not easy to put into practice. There is nothing wrong with still being on the path, not yet at the end.

The Course paints a stunningly beautiful picture of the real world and of Heaven, to which we will return (because we never left). The Course is clear about our goal – the happy dream – yet I believe most of us still have some way to go before we will be living that full time.

Let's be honest.

The value of all those wonderful passages in the Course that describe Reality is to help us keep our eye on the ball. We can derive enormous encouragement and inspiration from knowing our goal. But, so long as we are on the path of forgiveness that the Course maps out for us, we must not be tempted to skip steps, cut corners, or convince ourselves that we are where we are not.

Merely *understanding* that we never left Heaven is, as Werner Erhard said: "the booby prize". Being awake is not an *understanding* but *knowledge*, an experience. It means *living* there. The truth is that we have forgotten who we are. That's our only problem. But simply understanding that is not sufficient. It is like a man who suffers a blow to the head and loses his memory. He may understand what has happened from what the doctor tells him, but he still cannot remember anything about his life prior to the accident. He may be told that he has a family, a home, a job and a position in society. He understands and believes what he is told because he trusts the doctor, but he cannot remember for himself. We are like that – and remembering is a process that takes time.

Most of us will experience strong resistance to letting go of our self-concepts and awakening to the memory of God's love in our minds. Personally, I find it very helpful to look at my resistance, *"the obstacles to peace"* (Text, pp. 406–24), so I can surrender them to the Holy Spirit. The Course is about undoing the blocks to that memory.

What we are called upon to do is to see and know our goal, to know that truth is true and always will be so, yet to be honest about the stage we are at. We must hold both thoughts in our minds – Truth, in the ultimate sense, and also acceptance of the particular point we have reached on our *"journey without distance."* (Text, p. 150)

We then know the direction we are heading. We can have faith that we will reach our goal. In the meantime, we can rejoice at how far we have come. And we can be gentle and kind to ourselves.

On the way, we will get flashes of memory of the truth, "holy instants", and we can have faith that with the Holy Spirit's assistance, these instants will become more frequent. The experience of the forgiven world will become more familiar to us with patience and practice.

Oh, how the ego would love to think that it has reached the goal already – "I'm enlightened, so I must be wonderful." On the other hand, it would love to berate you for not being there, for not being good enough.

Neither is true. Be kind *and* be honest.

Forget not once this journey is begun the end is certain. Doubt along the way will come and go and go to come again. Yet is the ending sure... When you forget, remember that you walk with Him and with His Word upon your heart... Illusions of despair may seem to come, but learn how not to be deceived by them. Behind each one there is reality and there is God.
(Manual, p. 91)

Being Real and Innocent

Once we have read *A Course in Miracles* and practised the lessons, we might intellectually understand that we are as innocent and as holy as God created us. Understanding the truth of those good-news statements in the Course might make us feel good for a while. We might even have genuine moments of spiritual connection, holy instants, little revelations. But do we actually live there, all day, day in and day out? If we do not, then we still have work to do. And that work is, in Course terms, forgiveness, in all its rich and diverse shades of meaning.

I've written earlier about the need for honesty; there really is no other starting point for any of us. It is tempting for students of ACIM and other spiritual paths to 'spiritualise', by which I mean painting a pink, pseudo-spiritual gloss on painful issues and difficult situations. You know what I mean: Somebody does something terrible, and we respond "But we're all innocent Children of God" or "It's just an illusion." These may be true statements at one level. At another, they are just ideas in our head that are contradicted by gut feelings of wanting to punish, or get even. Those denied attack thoughts leak out in subtle ways, which others will feel, and we will experience in terms of increased guilt.

This substitution of an *illusion* of spirituality in place of the real thing was addressed often by Kenneth Wapnick. He emphasised the imperative of looking honestly at the ego, stressing that the denial of the ego's ugliness prevents genuine healing. For what is not uncovered cannot be brought to the light. In truth, it is our resistance to letting go that often drives our lives. To protect the ego's dream of individuality, we choose not to avail ourselves of the very means of our awakening.

The means of that awakening is forgiveness, acceptance, or giving up judgement of others and of ourselves. Once we have looked within, with honesty and courage, we are ready for forgiveness and release.

Really, not forgiving or accepting is insane. It flies in the face of 'what is'. I heard Byron Katie speak about this. All our pain, she said, comes from not accepting "what is". We need to accept what is, *because it is*.

In truth, what other choice do we have than to accept that we are the way we are, others are the way they are, our past was the way it was and the future will be what it will be? Otherwise, we are like a dog refusing to walk, being dragged along by its owner. The dog would have a much easier time if it just surrendered to the inevitable and went, willingly, with its owner – because it is going anyway – eventually!

With non-acceptance come the judgements and projections of guilt which the ego loves – and which keep us in hell. With acceptance and non-judgement comes peace. Let the Will of God be done.

"Yes, I want to kill my mother/kids/partner/best friend/boss. It's okay to feel what I feel, because I feel it." "I can accept that Fred is the way Fred is, because that's the way he is. I don't have to judge him for it. And if I do, that's okay, too." If we can accept and forgive these thoughts and feelings, we are free.

Yes, we are innocent! And, now, we really *know* it!

The Truth Hurts

Don't you just hate it when people quote *A Course in Miracles* to you at the most inappropriate times?

A friend of mine used to live in a small Cotswold market town. During one of my visits, the town's annual fun fair was taking place in the main street. On Saturday night we took a walk around, looking at the various attractions. By far the most impressive of the rides was a giant wheel (the 'wheel of hell' I later called it), which filled the width of the street. It looked innocuous enough when we first saw it, as it wasn't moving. I even thought that the view from the top would be worth seeing. So, we decided to have a go.

As we approached, however, the wheel was in full motion – and I could hear the screams! Despite a severe case of cold feet, I did not want to provide any grounds for being called a wimp, so I plunged ahead. After all, my fear was not real, my friend reminded me.

We were seated in a flimsy cage, made of what seemed like nothing more than chicken wire. I was sitting next to the door, which was secured only by a single latch. The cage itself rotated on a spindle attached to the circumference of the giant wheel. Already my pulse was racing. As the wheel was turned to allow subsequent victims to be seated, we lurched forward and upward, leaving my stomach behind. Our cage swung alarmingly as we moved further round, higher and higher. I desperately wanted to get off, but it was too late for that.

When everyone was aboard, rotation got fully underway, moderately at first, but rapidly increasing. Our cage was already oscillating wildly, but as the big wheel reached full speed, it turned us in complete somersaults. The forces of acceleration followed by sudden deceleration were extraordinary as we spun around – up, over the top, down, sweeping the ground (often upside down) and up again – inexorably, intolerably, on and on.

I hung on for dear life, slumped in my seat with eyes closed. At any moment I expected the cage door to swing open or the spindle that attached us to the wheel to snap, sending us crashing into the hard, cold stone wall of the bank building opposite, which seemed only inches from our faces. It was one of those occasions when you desperately wish that time, the world and your life would just stop right there, in that moment, and allow you to be anywhere else. I was screaming "Stop, stop! I want to get off." I hated every second. Presumably those people on the ground thought we were enjoying ourselves!

"Don't worry, it's just an illusion," my friend screamed back. "Your fear is not real." I wanted to kill him. Even the rational thought that this wheel of hell had presumably passed a safety inspection did not ease my terror. Despite my friend's taunts, I was convinced that my fears were justified and I was approaching overload.

Other times of sheer terror that I can recall, like jumping out of a perfectly good aeroplane at two thousand feet, lasted for only a few seconds. This one did not let up. I was treated to a full five minutes of unadulterated horror, which felt like forever, before the wheel slowed to a blissful halt and we staggered, dazed, into the crowd of bystanders.

My friend later admitted to having been as petrified as I was. But, in terms of *A Course in Miracles*, what he was saying was perfectly true. My fear was just an illusion. That fact can be demonstrated by a simple experiment. If I had been fully hypnotised and told to feel no fear, I would not have done so. Fear is not an absolute and immutable result of our circumstances.

However, in the midst of my experience, I was not ready to hear that. It is perfectly true that at any moment I could have changed my mind and have been totally at peace. But my belief in, and attachment to, the 'reality' of my situation and its inherent danger was so great that I did not choose to do so. It was clear that I was attached to my illusory life and the desire not to have my illusory body smashed to a pulp against the wall!

I know that my friend was simply engaging in bravado and teasing me, rather than trying to be unkind. But it can be tempting to misuse spiritual principles in this way. This kind of level confusion results in increasing guilt for others and ourselves. Like telling someone dying of cancer that their tumour is an illusion, it is less than helpful.

The truth is that we have made the world and its dangers seemingly real. Thus, it is more helpful to give ourselves and others a break, until such time as we are ready for metaphysical leaps of faith.

Other People – Our Perfect Mirrors

People are difficult, are they not? If only they would not be that way, or do those things! They are really annoying, frustrating and problematic. Life would be so much better and *we* would be so much happier and more peaceful if only *they* would be different, right?

No, unfortunately not! Despite what we may be tempted to believe, this is not the way it works. *A Course in Miracles* tells us that our problems with other people are actually telling us something about *ourselves*. If we have an issue with someone and are seeing them as guilty, then they are only mirroring something in ourselves that we feel guilty about, consciously or unconsciously.

That does not mean that they are not accountable for their actions, but it does mean that it is none of our business. We are only responsible for our *reaction* to it and, if it is an issue for us, if it 'pushes our buttons', then it says more about us – about our mistaken, negative beliefs about ourselves – than others.

One time, I was struggling with a friend. My problem was that she was being continually argumentative, snappy, dismissive and ungrateful for everything I did to help. Then, one day, I had a phone call from her. "Ian, we have to talk." My heart sank. "I have found you very difficult to be around," she added. "You always seem to be criticising whatever I do, and I never get any thanks from you." Here was my perfect mirror! We had both been projecting on to one another and now had the opportunity to let our grievances go.

This interaction brought about a powerful healing, but our challenges may not always be as clear-cut. But, although the grievance may take a different *form*, the *content* of the projected beliefs, what the situation *means* about them and us, will be the same.

The Course says:

Only the self-accused condemn... You never hate your brother for his sins, but only for your own.
(Text, p. 651)

The following story also illustrates how projection works:

A man named Harry went to his neighbour Sally's house to borrow her lawnmower. On his way to her house, he began to imagine how the conversation would go. He could 'hear' her in his mind, berating him for all the times he had been late in returning things, complaining about things he had returned broken or with missing pieces and generally berating him as unworthy of the loan of her lawnmower. He began to argue with the Sally in his head, pointing out all the things he had loaned her (including the time she had lost his biggest ladder and he did not even complain about it), but all to no avail – the Sally in his head would not let up.

Finally, he arrived at Sally's house and rang the doorbell. "What can I do for you?" a delighted Sally said as she welcomed her friend and neighbour. "You can keep your bloody lawnmower!" Harry screamed, slamming the door in the Sally's stunned face as he stormed away. (Adapted from *You Can Have What You Want* by Michael Neill.)

The value of encountering our own projections on to others is that we are able to know what is held unconscious in our own minds. Without other people to act as mirrors, we would not have the opportunity of seeing ourselves. We have no need, like Freud, to analyse our dreams to learn the secrets of our unconscious minds if we are alert enough to do it in our waking dreams.

This is the essence of forgiveness. As we forgive the other person's apparent guilt, we forgive our own because it is the same.

A shadow figure who attacks becomes a brother giving you a chance to help, if this becomes the function of the dream. And dreams of sadness thus are turned to joy.
(Text, p. 613)

Why Do We Project?

Underlying the whole ego thought system – that is, our ordinary, unforgiving thought processes – are the concepts of sin and guilt.

Originally, the idea of sin arose from the erroneous belief that we had separated from God. This is the Course's equivalent of the "original sin" of the Bible. Our experience was as if we had killed God, or broken up the perfect unity of Heaven. Not surprisingly, this resulted in feelings of the most terrible guilt. Imagine the guilt you would feel if you murdered your biological father or mother, then multiply that many times over!

How could we cope with such devastating guilt? The ego has provided two strategies: denial and projection. First, the ego tries to ignore the feeling and cover it up with layer upon layer of denial. This is like sweeping it under the carpet. But, like sweeping anything under the carpet, this doesn't work because nothing has really gone away. There is always some awareness of what is being denied. So, the ego comes up with its second strategy: projection.

In projection, the ego says: "The guilt is not in me, it's in you." We project the guilt from ourselves on to the nearest target – partner, parents, boss, the world – on to anybody really, as long as we get it as far away from us as possible. This is the origin of the word 'scapegoat'. In the Jewish tradition, the scapegoat was seen as a burden-carrying animal on which one could place one's sins and guilt. The scapegoat was seen as providing a spiritual service – like a pack animal for sins. The scapegoat carried away guilt for you.

Guilt, in the Course, is the sum total of all our negative feelings about ourselves: feelings of worthlessness, of not being good enough, of lack and emptiness. So, in projection, we say: "I am not the cause of my own bad feelings, you are."

But, again, projection does not work. We cannot successfully project guilt on to another without feeling guilty for doing *that* as well. So we end up feeling even worse. Projection of guilt simply compounds the problem – which is what the ego wanted all along, since your absorption with guilt is what keeps the ego going.

And indeed, this is what makes the world go round. We replay this scenario over and over again, in small ways and large ways, every day of our lives. This is how the ego advises us to think – and, mostly, we do. We can observe it not only in our daily relationships, but also in the arenas of politics and international relations.

So, now we can see that the negative qualities we accuse others of demonstrating are nothing less than the qualities we have denied in ourselves and projected on to them. We have actually peopled our lives with the projected contents of our own subconscious minds. I am not talking about the *actions* of others, but the *meaning* that we project on to their actions. The world is like a giant cinema screen, with our minds as the movie projector and our guilt the film running through it.

That's all well and good, but of what help is it to know this, you may ask? The beauty of it is that the Holy Spirit's answer lies in the very mechanism the ego has set up. The world is our 'magic mirror'. Without being able to see what is going on out there, on the movie screen of our lives, we would never know the contents of our minds that we have denied. Without the 'magic mirror' we would never have the chance of seeing and healing it. By forgiving the apparent guilt in others, we are actually forgiving it in ourselves – for the guilt we see in others *is* our own guilt.

Therefore, we can use a prayer such as the following from ACIM to release ourselves and our brother as one.

I give you to the Holy Spirit as part of myself. I know that you will be released, unless I want to use you to imprison myself. In the

name of my freedom I choose your release, because I recognize that we will be released together.
(Text, p. 329)

Eventually, by forgiving everyone in our lives, we can undo every fragment of guilt in our own minds. What a beautiful gift!

Our Function as "The Light"

Life can get really busy and complicated. I find that there are so many things to do – plans, arrangements, projects, goals, ambitions. Sometimes, just organising simple, day-to-day living can take up all your time!

The list of priorities can get pretty lengthy – friends, family, health, work and career, shopping, holidays, banking and bills, cooking, housecleaning and repairs. Even entertainment and relaxation can be stressful. Just when am I going to find the time for all of it?

All this activity can seem so important, as if this is somehow what our lives are about. Yet is that actually true? What are we really here for? What is the purpose of our lives?

There is a series of lessons (Lessons 61–66) in *A Course in Miracles* that give us more than a clue about our true purpose. In fact, by merely reading the headings of those six lessons, we can be fairly clear on what the Course's intention is for us.

"I am the light of the world."

"Forgiveness is my function as the light of the world."

"The light of the world brings peace to every mind through my forgiveness."

"Let me not forget my function."

"My only function is the one God gave me." And...

"My happiness and my function are one."

As children of God, our experience of anything other than that truth is what we have invented about ourselves. To be anything other than the light of Love simply means that we have forgotten the Truth. When we believe that we are these busy people living in the world and attending to all these activities, we have forgotten.

So what, then, is the "function of the light of the world"? It is to forgive others and, therefore, ourselves (since minds are joined) that we may experience the truth and remember that we *are* that light.

Lesson 62 says that we do not forgive because we do not realise what forgiveness will do for us – namely that it *"will resolve all sense of weakness, strain... fatigue... fear... guilt and pain...* [and] *restore the invulnerability and power of God"* to us. (Workbook, p. 104)

The purpose of the world is to tempt us to forget our function, luring us into its dramas and busyness. Yet I am not saying that we must change anything we currently do in the world. Whatever we do and however busy we are, we can remember that our purpose, in everything, is to awaken to the experience of who we truly are – the Light.

The world will present us with many temptations to forget, to attack, or to justify unforgiveness. We do not realise that, in so doing, we attack ourselves. Every time we succumb to that temptation, our function is to remember again what the lesson is in each situation, and what learning that lesson will bring us. Our function is to *be* the Light in our daily busyness. Only that way will we find lasting peace and happiness, the surrender of illusions, and the salvation of the world by that demonstration. *"Be happy, for your only function here is happiness."* (Workbook, p. 184)

Sometimes, our problems seem so real and difficult that we may be tempted to think we have succumbed to failure and disaster. Yet it is in those moments – within those very thoughts – that the turning points in our salvation are to be found. That's because we *will* falter, stumble and fall from time to time. Yet in every difficult circumstance, we can find what there is to learn and grow from – what the lesson is – and pick ourselves up. If there is one thing I know from my years on the spiritual path, it is that I make mistakes and they are sometimes painful. Yet this is the classroom I have chosen. What I learn from such situations *is* the purpose and function of my life. If not that, then what else?

Only Love Is Real

"Only love is real." Although this is not an exact quote from the Course, it is the essential message. It is another of the Course's concepts that is difficult for us to accept in our everyday lives. We ask: "How can *only* love be real?" "What about this feeling, or that problem?" Our pain certainly feels real when we are experiencing it. So we try telling ourselves: "Don't worry about that, it's not real!" And then we wonder why we continue to feel the pain. How can our anger, hurt, guilt, loss and fear not be real when we are right there, immersed in it? How can someone else's attack not be real? After all, whatever they did is undeniable: "I know it's true. I have witnesses!"

It is really impossible to explain logically how powerfully negative experiences are not real, in a way that the world would understand. We might understand this concept intellectually, but experiencing it as true is quite another matter.

However, I begin to feel the truth of this principle operating in my life when I look back to my feelings in past situations. When I am having a painful experience, such as a dispute with someone, falling out, feeling attacked or let down, I tend to lose myself in the drama of the situation and forget who I am and why I am here. That is, I forget that I am Love and that I am here only *to* love. But I can remember to call on the Holy Spirit to correct my thinking and return me to my right mind through forgiveness. Once my peace of mind has been restored, the circumstances which caused the upset always look very different. In retrospect, I often ask myself: "What was that all about anyway?" Sometimes I cannot even remember what I was fighting about.

At worst, the dispute appears to have been a misunderstanding or a mistake, but usually it looks like *nothing*; in other words, it wasn't even real. *All that is left is the love I feel for the other person involved.* And this is a clue to what was really going on. In this frame of mind, my right mind, I can see that 'only the love was real' and the rest was illusion. When someone moves out of my life, for whatever reason – a relationship breaks up, someone moves away, or someone dies – a similar experience takes place.

For example, a friend of fifteen years standing recently emigrated to New Zealand. My first reaction was as if she had died! But I recognise that the love that I once felt for people who are no longer in my life is still there. I feel the love, now, every bit as much as I did when they were around, if not more so. Here again is another clue to what is the Truth. Once more, I can begin to see that 'only the love is real'. Time and distance are but illusions too.

'Only love is real.' I believe this is the Truth that lies behind all the illusions of this world. Once I have forgiven, only love remains.

You will find this place of truth [where you will to unite with God] *as you see it in your brothers, for though they may deceive themselves, like you they long for the grandeur that is in them. And perceiving it you will welcome it, and it will be yours. For grandeur is the right of God's Son, and no illusions can satisfy him or save him from what he is. Only his love is real, and he will be content only with his reality.*
(Text, p. 244)

Inner Peace, Not World Peace

Let us consider how a good student of *A Course in Miracles* should react to events in the world. How do we deal with what we see on the news or read in the newspapers? Should we even *be* watching the news or reading the papers? How can we keep our peace when there is so much war and violence out there? Maybe it is best to ignore it all. Or maybe we should be praying to save the world.

The peace that *A Course in Miracles* offers does not necessarily mean a world without wars. It does not mean a world where nothing terrible ever happens, or where no problems appear to exist. The Course offers, instead, a route to *inner* peace, a place in the mind where we are at peace regardless of what is going on in what appears to be the outer world. It is not for nothing that the publisher of *A Course in Miracles* is the "Foundation for Inner Peace" instead of a "Foundation for World Peace".

It is a commonly held idea that ACIM students should be praying for world peace, for an end to war. But wars happen because war exists in our minds, collectively and individually. Just as charity begins at home, so too does peace begin there – in our own minds, that is. Does this mean that we ignore what is going on in the world, pretend we do not care when we do, or even pretend that there is no war when bombs are being dropped? After all, the Course says that the world is an illusion, right?

No. I believe that our old friend known as "level confusion" has got in our way again. It would seem to me that it's a loving act to stop a school bully from beating up a smaller child, even if it was necessary to use force and inflict physical pain on the bully to bring about a halt to his actions. Or would we just stand around praying for them both?

Leaving aside geopolitics and military strategies, it could be regarded as a loving act to drop bombs on a "bully" who is inflicting suffering on a weaker people or nation, not as a punishment but if it might result in the overall saving of life and in the easing of human plight.

So, what we do with school bullies and genocidal dictators is the same. We endeavour to stop them the best way we know how. *And* we pray. Ideally, we do both simultaneously. But we pray, most of all, for our own peace of mind. Our aim is to be at peace even whilst being at war. Feeling that we have acted lovingly, or at least done the best we knew how, will naturally help that peace of mind. Ultimately, it is the role of the Holy Spirit to restore via forgiveness the peace of mind of which *A Course in Miracles* speaks.

Maybe there is no world, but that is not immediately relevant when we are faced with the school bully or a despotic megalomaniac. If peace begins at home, I believe that it is only the establishment of peace in our minds that will bring about world peace. After all, the world is in our minds.

Conversely, I do not believe that avoiding the negativity of the news preserves our peace of mind. This evasive stance subtly affirms that there is something *real* and terrible out there, and something that we must get away from. None of this is so. Healing is not avoidance. Healing cannot be accomplished if what needs healing is not first looked at, thoroughly, gently and lovingly.

So how does the good student of *A Course in Miracles* respond to world events? He does not ignore them; he simply looks and judges not. He acts as lovingly as possible in any given circumstance. He remembers the holy Presence in his own mind as he prays to reclaim his own peace of mind.

Disclaiming Victimhood

One of the most challenging ideas in *A Course in Miracles* is summed up by Lesson 31: *"I am not the victim of the world I see"* (Workbook, p. 48). Because it does seem as if we are subject to innumerable forces and circumstances that impinge on our peace of mind.

I imagine we all believe that we would be happier if only things would go the way we think they should, and if people would behave in the way we want. I have long since realised that I can choose my response to all life's problems and dramas, but what ACIM says goes way beyond that:

> *The world you see depicts exactly what you thought you did. Except that now you think that what you did is being done to you. The guilt for what you thought is being placed outside yourself, and on a guilty world... It brings its vengeance, not your own.*
> (Text, p. 587)

Think about it: when a problem arises, what do you tend to think about? Do you secretly believe that living in the world is just one big problem, or that you're getting what you deserve? Either way, these are beliefs that the world seems to confirm for you. When situations at work do not go according to plan, when people in my life let me down and I am seemingly abandoned yet again, these circumstances perfectly reflect my state of mind and my beliefs.

The Course says that we forget we are the dreamer and identify with a figure in the dream, believing that is who we are. Thus we have cause and effect reversed. Our thoughts are the cause; the world is the effect.

We believe in separation, in a cause that is untrue and impossible. The physical world reflects none of the attributes of God, so cannot be His Creation. It is merely the effect of that erroneous thought.

If we will allow it, the Holy Spirit will show us it is impossible that anything be done to us without our will, and we can be free of a cause that never was.

> ... let us merely look upon the dream's beginning, for the part you see is but the second part, whose cause lies in the first... In gentle laughter does the Holy Spirit perceive the cause, and looks not to effects. How else could He correct your error, who have overlooked the cause entirely? He bids you bring each terrible effect to Him that you may look together on its foolish cause and laugh with Him a while... And by His judgment are effects removed.
> (Text, pp. 586–7)

We cannot do this alone. We need help from outside our problematic belief system. This is the Holy Spirit's role. He will help us forgive all situations if we will let him. *"When you forgive the world your guilt, you will be free of it."* (Text, p. 588)

The Holy Spirit will correct our errors and reversed thinking. If we offer each situation to Him, we can begin to laugh with Him as the cause is removed. Whatever the many forms our problems take,

> ... He would teach you but the single cause of all of them... And you will understand that miracles reflect the simple statement, "I have done this thing, and it is this I would undo."
> (Text, p. 588)

Then we will experience ourselves not as separate from the world and from our brothers, but as innocent as they are, and at one with them. Thus we can achieve a complete reversal of the victim thought system of the world.

What keeps the world in chains but your beliefs?... The world is nothing in itself. Your mind must give it meaning. And what you behold upon it are your wishes, acted out so you can look on them and think them real... There is no world apart from what you wish, and herein lies your ultimate release. Change but your mind on what you want to see, and all the world must change accordingly. (Workbook, p. 242)

Four Approaches to the Course

Looking at the variety of articles published in *Miracle Worker* magazine over the years and reviewing all the events we've held, I have noticed four basic approaches to the Course. Perhaps each of these represents a successive advancement on the spiritual path. That is not to say that one approach is better than another. They each have value. We would not reach the later stages of the journey without travelling the earlier ones. Yet, if we remain at the beginning, we miss the gifts offered later on.

The first approach is *intellectual*, focused on explanations of the Course's principles, discussions of what a particular passage means and analysis of concepts. Often this activity is denigrated as being too 'mental' or scholarly, and people focused on this approach may be told by others that they are too much 'in their heads'. But I'd suggest that the Course, being a book of 1,250 pages, is meant to be studied and analysed, to some extent. How can we expect to apply the ideas and obtain the necessary experience if we do not comprehend what we are attempting to apply?

The second approach is *inspirational*. One might feel inspired by a particular passage or idea from the Course – uplifted, excited and motivated. The effect is usually transitory; one can awake the next day and feel the same as usual, if not actually deflated. However, this kind of inspiration still has value, as it can be enough to shift our thinking and keep us on the path.

The third approach is what I will call *situational*. It includes those teachings and activities that help us deal with whatever particular situation we're facing in the moment, whether it's a relationship issue, a problem at work, or a challenge to our self-esteem. These situations may be dealt with in a number of ways, including asking for guidance, praying, following ACIM's *"Rules for Decision"* (Text, pp. 625–9), or using this prayer: *"I must have decided wrongly, because I am not at peace...* " (Text, p. 90). Forgiveness always makes relationships go more smoothly and easily, resolving conflicts and sorting out disagreements. Obviously, there is value in anything that helps life work better and improves relationships.

However, I think the fourth approach is what the Course is really about and where the other approaches lead. This is the *transformational* aspect, in which we are fundamentally changed by the healing of our minds. This is the ultimate purpose of forgiveness. Once transformation has taken place, issues that caused us to lose our peace before no longer do so, or they no longer occur because we've released that particular aspect of guilt in our minds to project on to the world. Over time, as our minds heal in this way, the ego thought system is undone. Eventually we attain what the Course calls the "happy dream", which is the final step before we awaken for good.

Problems As Opportunities

Problems, problems, problems! Life seems to present us with a never-ending series of hurdles, difficulties and utter disasters, does it not? Well, actually, no!

One of the most important gifts of *A Course in Miracles* is an overarching context for my life. It helped me to realise that everything in my life happens for a purpose. And I've learned that I can choose the purpose of anything that occurs. I can choose that it serve the ego's purpose – to keep me stuck in pain and turmoil – or I can use it for the Holy Spirit's purpose, as an opportunity for learning and growth.

There is nothing that can happen to us that cannot be seen as holding a gift or a miracle within it – once we change our minds. To the Holy Spirit, therefore, there are no problems, only opportunities.

For example, I taught a workshop in Norway once. Having worked out the details several months before, I was all set to go when I learned, two days before my departure, that a residential weekend had been arranged and that the participants' lodging and food for two days were to be financed by their workshop fees. Only what was left, after these considerable expenses, would be paid to me and my co-facilitator. Consequently, we would receive only a small fraction of what we had expected.

I was shocked, angry, and bewildered. When I told the Norwegian promoter how I was feeling, she asked if I wanted to cancel the weekend. Without hesitation, I replied that we would be there and that I was sure it would work out. I was determined to see this differently and to accept the situation regardless – but I still felt sick. I felt it would take a while to forgive the mix-up and poor communication.

It turned out that the retreat centre was beautiful, located amongst wooded hills southwest of Oslo. It had been snowing and the setting was idyllic. The fourteen participants were delightful, the food provided was wonderful and the workshop was a great success. I had an excellent weekend, a real gift.

On the Sunday night following the workshop, the promoter invited my co-facilitator and me into her stunning home, where we stayed for two days. That night I sat with her to discuss the financial issue that had arisen. We both shared how we felt about the events five days earlier. As I heard her speak of how ashamed she felt and how much she believed she had failed by not informing me what was being planned and how it would affect us, my heart went out to her. I melted. Suddenly, I felt nothing but warmth, empathy and closeness to her. It was a beautiful moment of joining – my second gift.

I could have continued to see the situation as a problem, even as a disaster, and thus been closed to the miracles and healing opportunities available. I am grateful that I chose to see it differently and to receive the gifts that were the inevitable result of changing my mind.

The ego and the Holy Spirit are two parts of our minds and they are mutually exclusive. The ego is not a malevolent being; it is merely a fearful belief we hold. It is part of us that we can choose for or against. It is up to us to decide which we listen to. Problems are opportunities to forgive, love and remember the truth. Maybe we can even begin to welcome problems for what they offer us, rather than dread them.

You have no problems that He cannot solve by offering you a miracle.
(Text, p. 298)

Perception's Challenge

Someone wrote to me complaining about a teacher advertising in *Miracle Worker* who was charging "£300 per hour to be in his spiritual presence." That didn't sound right to me; I couldn't remember any such thing, so I enquired. When she gave me the teacher's name, I looked back and saw the actual price quoted in the advert was, in fact, fifteen pounds for thirty minutes of one-to-one counselling. That was quite a different matter, yet the reader was convinced that she was right.

This reminded me of the unreliability of perception. What we are convinced is there, or that someone has said or done, may be radically different from what others perceive or what really occurred. The police often find that if they obtain statements from ten witnesses to an accident, they will get ten different versions of events.

Many years ago, when I was at university, I believed some friends had not invited me to their student party. I felt hurt, betrayed and abandoned, and a number of old emotional wounds were triggered. I reacted angrily to these events. Though I was absolutely convinced I had been deliberately shunned, much later I learned that the truth was quite different. My invitation had merely been lost; what I thought had happened had not. However, the damage had been done because my reaction was then misinterpreted and some untrue stories about me went around. I hasten to add that this is not just my ego putting on what the Course calls a false *"face of innocence"* (Text, pp. 656–8). Almost all of what was said was factually incorrect or, at least, open to question – and yet was believed to be true.

The problem is that we perceive what is not there. My interpretation of events was certainly untrue and so were the others' reactive views of me. When was it not ever thus, in this world?

A Course in Miracles says that our perception is never objective.

It will *always* be incorrect to some degree. That's because the ego sees what it has already decided it is going to see, and then only sees evidence that proves its beliefs are correct. The Course asserts that this is not seeing at all!

Each of your perceptions of 'external reality' is a pictorial represen-tation of your own attack thoughts. One can well ask if this can be called seeing. Is not fantasy a better word for such a process, and hallucination a more appropriate term for the result?
(Workbook, p. 34)

No evidence will convince you of the truth of what you do not want.
(Text, p. 333)

For eyes and ears are senses without sense, and what they see and hear they but report. It is not they that hear and see, but you, who put together every jagged piece, each senseless scrap and shred of evidence, and make a witness to the world you want.
(Text, pp. 601–2)

These are the criteria we use for judgement. So, next time you are a tempted to believe you know what another has said or done, and what this means about them, or you, pause a moment and ask yourself, as Byron Katie would: "Is it true?" and then "Can you absolutely know that it's true?"

A friend sent me a card once which sums it all up: "I know you believe you understood what you think I said, but I am not sure you realise that what you heard is not what I meant."

Forgiving the Not-Done

Forgiveness is not about forgiving someone for what they have done; it is about forgiving them for what they have *not* done. Forgiving them for what they seem to have done is what the Course calls *"forgiveness-to-destroy"* (Song of Prayer, pp. 11–12). It amounts to saying that what they did was real, but you are big enough to let them off the hook.

Real forgiveness is recognising that there is nothing to forgive, because they did not do anything. What they *appeared* to do was an illusion, in the form of your projection. You may think that what they did *had* to be real. After all, you may have scars to prove it! But, in truth, you hired that person, wrote the script for them and directed their performance. They are simply mirroring back to you your beliefs about yourself.

You know that in your sleeping dreams you can appear to be attacked and you can feel fear, without actually being in danger. On waking you realise that the experience, however real it felt, was just a dream and that you were safe in bed the whole time. The waking dreams of everyday life are the same. We can give and experience full-on, Oscar-worthy performances; we can feel the adrenaline rush of fear and be fully involved in our dreams, but it doesn't make them any more real than our sleeping dreams. All the time, we were safe at Home.

Forgiveness undoes our projections by reminding us that what appeared to happen never happened in reality. It means seeing our brother's innocence even if circumstances *appear* to make them responsible for destroying our peace of mind.

All that is happening is mind exposing itself; your beliefs are being revealed to you through your experience. We can even learn to be grateful for all our experiences, positive and negative – for how else would we know what our beliefs are and which perceptions need healing?

Forgiveness is seeing our brothers as God sees them, wholly innocent in truth. (Incidentally, we must not get caught up here in "level confusion" and attempt to deny our ordinary experience. A criminal can be guilty in the eyes of the law, but still be innocent in the eyes of God.) It is our arrogance that lets us believe that we can judge guilty whom God has judged innocent.

Forgiveness undoes the illusory world of guilt, blame and attack, where we feel guilty and deserving of punishment. Blaming others simply makes *us* feel guilty; it reinforces our feelings of guilt about ourselves. By seeing our brothers' innocence, we are reminded of our own.

When you are tempted to believe that sin is real, remember this: If sin is real, both God and you are not. If creation is extension, the Creator must have extended Himself, and it is impossible that what is part of Him is totally unlike the rest. If sin is real, God must be at war with Himself. He must be split, and torn between good and evil; partly sane and partly insane. For He must have created what wills to destroy Him, and has the power to do so. Is it not easier to believe that you have been mistaken to believe in this?
(Text, p. 405)

God Knows Us Not

If the world is an illusion, as *A Course in Miracles* states, and God does not even know about what goes on here, in our dream, then are we totally alone and to whom can we pray? This idea can leave people thinking that there is no one to whom they can turn. There are various ways of looking at this conundrum, all of which are true.

On one level, it is understandable that we feel alone here. We do not feel at home in the world because it is *not* our home. We are longing for God and our *true* home, which we may faintly remember; the *"Forgotten Song"* (Text, p. 445) of the Course is not quite forgotten. However, it is loneliness and the deep longing for home that often prompts our spiritual search.

It is also true that, in reality, we are still at home in Heaven. We have not gone anywhere because it is impossible for a part of God to be separate from Him. We are just dreaming a dream of being here, like a child in bed having a nightmare. The contents of the dream seem very real when the child is dreaming but, on waking, it is clear that nothing really happened. The spiritual journey is a process of awakening from that dream to find that we have been at home all along. This is more than an intellectual understanding of illusion; eventually we *experience* awakening to reality outside the dream.

In the same way that a parent does not know the content of a child's dream, only that it is dreaming, God does not know the content of *our* dream, what seems to be going on here in the world of time and space. He would have to fall asleep and start hallucinating, too, and He doesn't do that. He knows only the Truth. So, God did not make the physical world of time, space and bodies; *we* did when we collectively fell asleep. And it's good news that God has nothing to do with all this. If He *did*, that would make it real and all our misperceptions about ourselves would be true. All the disasters and the cruelty in the world would be real. We would be here with no way out, nothing better to awaken to. God would be cruel indeed.

Why don't we just wake up, then? Because we *like* it here – the world of our individuality, our specialness – even though it brings us pain. The Course defines the ego as the part of our minds that mistakenly believes in the reality of all this. Our resistance to waking up is the ego's fear of annihilation. Waking up to the Oneness of Heaven would be the end of the ego and the ego knows that, so it lies to us that it can offer something better. And it tells us we will be punished if we return home – punished for running away. That is the story of the Prodigal Son. In fact, we too will be welcomed with open arms by our Father.

Once a parent realises the child is having a nightmare, it tries to wake the child up, calling, "Wake up. It's just a dream. You're safe." If the sleeping child hears the parent's voice and listens, the child may begin to wake up. This Voice calling to us in *our* dream is the Holy Spirit, which we can choose to listen to, and begin to awaken. That's why He is called the Voice for God in the Course.

But the Holy Spirit is more active than merely a voice in the dream. The Course says the Holy Spirit knows both the Truth of God and *"He perceives* [the illusion] *because He was sent to save humanity."* (Manual for Teachers, p. 89) So, He may actively guide us within our dream. He is the correction, the Atonement principle, the bringer of true perception in this world, yet *"He never forgets the Creator or His Creation* [who we truly are]." (Manual, p. 89)

He is also the connection, the *"communication link between God and His separated Sons"* (Text, p. 151 and Manual, p. 89) the presence of which proves that we are not really separate from God (the parent who is still in the room). We are not alone; it's just a mistaken belief.

Finally, to whom do we pray? Strictly speaking, to the Holy

Spirit since He hears us and we can hear Him as the Voice for God. In practice, I don't think it matters whom we pray to, or what name we use. I don't think the Holy Spirit says: "He is calling to God, so it's nothing to do with me. I'll ignore him!" It is your *intention* to connect with the Truth that matters, not the words or names you use.

You are a child of God, a priceless part of His Kingdom, which He created as part of Him. Nothing else exists and only this is real. You have chosen a sleep in which you have had bad dreams, but the sleep is not real and God calls you to awake. There will be nothing left of your dream when you hear Him, because you will awaken... When you wake you will see the truth around you and in you, and you will no longer believe in dreams because they will have no reality for you. Yet the Kingdom and all that you have created there will have great reality for you, because they are beautiful and true.
(Text, pp. 101–2)

The Presence of God and Love

A Course in Miracles tells us that its purpose is the removal of the blocks to the awareness of love's presence (which is also the presence of God). These blocks, common to all of us, are the beliefs in sin, guilt, fear, anger, attack and judgement. These beliefs keep the ego in business.

I have been doing a lot of work on myself, exploring and transforming some of the particular ways I have played out these deep-rooted beliefs in my life. That work involves the healing of my perceptions about myself and my relationships.

In this chapter I'm sharing some of my process with you because I know that to teach is to learn. I've made the commitment to remind myself that I am not a victim and that my salvation does not come from outside myself. My goal is to find strength and peace within, rather than to expect people and circumstances to follow my dictates. My goal is to be at peace regardless of externals.

Specifically, I am healing my unfinished business with my mother. I mistakenly believed that she abandoned me at the age of two and a half in favour of looking after my younger brother when he was born. Since then, I have often seen myself as being alone, separate and essentially different from others. I came to believe that, since I did not fit in, there must be something wrong with me. I tend to project my mother on to other women, believing that they will abandon me, leading me to keep my distance from them in order to stay safe.

I am working on my unfinished business with my brother, too, with whom I have been in competition since he was born. I relive constantly the moment of fear, when I believed that something was going on between my mother and brother of which I was not a part, reinforcing my feelings of being separate and left out. I find myself in competition with other men for others' attention. I project my brother on to other men and find myself in admiration of them, perceiving them as being better than me. This leads me into difficulty around sexuality, since I confuse the admiration I feel towards these men with attraction. This is really an attraction to guilt.

Realising that something was going on for me, my mother tried to 'fix' me by urging me to be like my brother: confident, extroverted, good with people and so on. But this reinforced the idea that I was not acceptable as I was, also intensifying my sense of competition.

I also want to heal my unfinished business with my father, who I perceived as being emotionally absent and physically undemonstrative. I tend to project my father on to other men and long for intimacy from them.

I have committed to heal the following beliefs about myself and make new choices:

1. Whenever I attempt to prove that I have been rejected, I am really reinforcing my belief that I deserve to be alone – and I choose to feel connected and one with everyone.
2. Whenever I attempt to prove that people around me are unreliable, I am really reinforcing my belief that I deserve to be alone – and I choose to feel connected.
3. Whenever I attempt to prove that I am not good enough, I am reinforcing my belief that there is something wrong with me – and I choose to feel worthy and whole.
4. Whenever I attempt to prove that I am not loveable, I am reinforcing my belief that I deserve to be alone because I am not good enough – and I choose to feel worthy.
5. Whenever I do not ask for help, because asking for help would confirm the belief that I am not good enough, I choose to feel worthy.
6. Whenever I choose to stay alone and withdraw, I am really trying to show the world that I have had a hard life, that no

one understands me and that others reject me. I choose to feel connected and at one with my brothers.

7. Whenever I am tempted to believe that my diabetic condition will get worse, I am really attempting, again, to show the world that I have had a hard life and no one understands me. I choose to feel healthy and accepted.

Above all, I am asking the Holy Spirit to remind the wounded child in me, who made up the fundamental belief that he is alone, that he is not alone. I commit to forgiving myself for holding these mistaken beliefs and to forgive those I have blamed for being the cause. I do not want to become a lonely, sick old man (my biggest fear). By making these commitments, I am committing to a positive future.

Finally, I realise that in writing this section I have taken a risk, but I feel it is important, if I am taking the Course seriously, to demonstrate defencelessness and openness in all my relationships.

A Reasonable Analysis

I am a very intellectual person. I like to analyse, figure things out, come up with answers and organise things. The labels I give the things of the world include *good, bad, right, wrong, desirable, undesirable, worthy of me or unworthy of me,* and the like.

It seems reasonable to do this. We are taught that evaluating is normal behaviour. I built a career in the oil industry out of judging and so it's hard not to attempt to evaluate *everything.* Indeed, how could I survive in the world without discrimination, estimation and evaluation? The answer is that I cannot.

Do I not need these functions just to cross the road? Of course I do, but only because I believe that there is a road to cross. I believe that there are hard, speeding objects called cars that could come along and hurt or kill me. So long as I believe in the irresistible physical reality of the world, then I must believe in the necessity of judgement. But we know what *A Course in Miracles* says about the physical world: it does not exist. Therefore, where are my judgements now?

I believe that *"there is a hierarchy of illusions; some are more valuable"* and that there are *"degrees of truth among illusions..."* (Text, pp. 439–40) I must be insane! I have come to realise that, whether they be significant value judgements or minor discriminations, my judgements mean nothing in reality. In practice, too, they often get me nowhere. They lead me to more questions than answers. The analysis, organisation and labelling of everything leads only to more things which must be analysed, organised and labelled. It is tiring work – energy-sapping, diminishing and limiting.

Judgement leads to continual division, separation and cutting off. All judgement keeps me stuck in the illusion that judgement is both necessary and effective. Yet, I am frustrated when that proves untrue. What are my thoughts, my judgements? They are nothing.

A Course in Miracles says that the prerequisite for knowledge is to give up the idea that one actually knows anything:

> *... the thoughts of which you are aware... are not your real thoughts.*
> (Workbook, p. 16)

> *Nothing that you think are your real thoughts resemble your real thoughts in any respect.*
> (Workbook, p. 71)

My real thoughts lie elsewhere. The place of not-knowing, where I always end up anyway, is really a good place to be. If I give up on knowing, this allows a space for my real thoughts to be revealed.

> *My meaningless thoughts are showing me a meaningless world.*
> (Workbook, p. 18)

The answer is to give up my meaningless thoughts; in other words, to give up looking for meaning in my typical thoughts. There is none. I must allow those thoughts to be as they are, knowing what they are. I thereby create the space for the thoughts of God to show themselves.

> *To do nothing is to rest, and make a place within you where the activity of the body ceases to demand attention. Into this place the Holy Spirit comes, and there abides.*
> (Text, p. 390)

By the way, I assure you that everything I have written here is true... but then again, what do I know?!

The Lord's Prayer

My favourite passage from *A Course in Miracles* is essentially the Course's equivalent of the Lord's Prayer.

> *Forgive us our illusions, Father, and help us to accept our true relationship with You, in which there are no illusions, and where none can ever enter. Our holiness is Yours. What can there be in us that needs forgiveness when Yours is perfect? The sleep of forgetfulness is only the unwillingness to remember Your forgiveness and Your Love. Let us not wander into temptation, for the temptation of the Son of God is not Your Will. And let us receive only what You have given, and accept but this into the minds which You created and which You love. Amen.*
> (Text, p. 350)

The beauty of these words and the profundity of the message can move me to tears. Yet I also feel sad that the more familiar Lord's Prayer has been so often misunderstood through the centuries. I believe the Course is attempting to correct some of the misinterpretations of Christianity.

So what does this new form of the prayer mean?

The first line: *"Forgive us our illusions, Father"* suggests that we are asking God to forgive us. Yet elsewhere the Course says: *"God does not forgive because He has never condemned."* (Workbook, p. 73) He knows, then, that we do not need His forgiveness. Our prayers are never for the benefit of God, but for our own. We need our reminders. This line: *"Forgive us our illusions, Father"* reminds *us* of our innocence. Our illusions are all the false, negative beliefs we hold about ourselves.

The idea that this is about remembering our innocence is supported by the next three lines: *"... help us to accept our true relationship with You, in which there are no illusions, and where none can ever enter."* Our true relationship with God is that we are one with Him and, thus, totally free of illusions, that is, our seeming guilt, flaws, imperfections, lack and sense of unworthiness.

"Our holiness is Yours." Our holiness is God's because, as His Creations, we are like Him, absolutely whole and complete. *"What can there be in us that needs forgiveness when Yours is perfect?"* Again, this means that God knows Who we are. Again, He does not need to forgive us because He knows our innocence and perfection always; it is we who have fallen asleep and forgotten the truth. Believing the ego's lies about ourselves, we have become identified with the ego and are thus invested in hanging on to our guilt, at all costs – especially the great cost to our peace of mind. *"The sleep of forgetfulness is only the unwillingness to remember Your forgiveness and Your Love."* We have forgotten Who we are and thus the spiritual path is simply the process of remembering.

"Let us not wander into temptation, for the temptation of the Son of God is not Your Will." Here, we are not being warned against doing bad things; there is nothing here about sinning or trespassing. "Temptation" means merely the tendency to believe in illusions and forget the truth of who we are. *Let us not be tempted to forget.*

The prayer then encourages us to turn away from these illusions and accept *only* the truth of God's love for us. *"Let us receive only what You have given, and accept but this into the minds which You created and which You love."* This may be easier said than done! Yet the Course says that we need only "a little willingness" to receive the desired outcome: peace of mind.

I think this prayer moves me because it speaks to a part of me that wants to accept and remember the truth of God's love, above all else. I'm not often aware of this aspect of myself and this prayer allows me, however briefly, to access it.

Shakespearean Wisdom

From time to time, I do a bit of acting – nothing too serious. It's just 'am-dram' but I enjoy it. Theatre gets me out of my comfort zone, allowing me to exercise aspects of myself that are normally dormant.

I had always told myself to steer clear of Shakespeare; I preferred plays written in English! In 2008, however, I was offered parts in two of the Bard's plays and decided to take the plunge. As a result, I gained a new appreciation of this playwriting genius.

As well as being a playwright, Shakespeare was a philosopher who offered some profound insights into life and the human condition. One of my favourite speeches (which I used to quote, even while professing not to want to perform it) is from *Macbeth*, Act 5, Scene 5. Here Macbeth's plans are falling apart around him and he has just been informed that the Queen is dead. He famously says:

Life's but a walking shadow, a poor player
That struts and frets his hour upon the stage
And then is heard no more: it is a tale
Told by an idiot, full of sound and fury,
Signifying nothing.

Shakespeare knew that in this world, each of us is a "poor player", an actor playing roles. We may play many roles in our lives at the same time. Some of mine are: director of the Miracle Network, son, friend, godfather, residents' association member, walker and actor. But they are all merely roles I have taken on and believe in.

Good theatre and cinema induces what is known as 'suspension of disbelief', whereby we temporarily forget we are watching a play or movie and get totally lost in it, believing it to be real. The same applies to acting. A good actor becomes his character and loses himself.

In our lives, we think our roles are who we are, but they are no more real than Macbeth's "walking shadows". We get lost in our characters and in all the dramas our personalities become embroiled in, utterly engaged in our make-believe worlds. We "strut and fret [our] hour upon the stage", becoming "full of sound and fury", certain that we are right about who we are and that our perceptions are true, resistant to any suggestion of letting them go and embracing the Truth. We forget that this life is a "tale told by an idiot" who does not know Who he really is.

A Course in Miracles discusses this play-acting at length, notably in the section "The 'Hero' of the Dream":

> *The body is the central figure in the dreaming of the world... It takes the central place in every dream, which tells the story of how it was made by other bodies, born into the world outside the body, lives a little while and dies, to be united in the dust with other bodies dying like itself. In the brief time allotted it to live, it seeks for other bodies as its friends and enemies...*
>
> *The dreaming of the world takes many forms, because the body seeks in many ways to prove it is autonomous and real... It works to get [possessions], doing senseless things, and tosses them away for senseless things it does not need and does not even want. It hires other bodies, that they may protect it and collect more senseless things that it can call its own. It looks about for special bodies that can share its dream. Sometimes it dreams it is a conqueror of bodies weaker than itself. But in some phases of the dream, it is the slave of bodies that would hurt and torture it.*
>
> *The body's serial adventures, from the time of birth to dying, are the theme of every dream the world has ever had. The 'hero' of this dream will never change, nor will its purpose... This single lesson does it try to teach again, and still again, and yet once more; that it*

is cause and not effect. And you are its effect, and cannot be its cause.

Thus are you not the dreamer, but the dream. And so you wander idly in and out of places and events that it contrives... a figure in a dream. But who reacts to figures in a dream unless he sees them as if they were real? The instant that he sees them as they are they have no more effects on him...

(Text, pp. 585–6)

During my years of acting, I have become increasingly aware that my roles in plays are little different to my roles in life. I play my part, but they are no more real. It is important that we all recognise the scripts we are learning and reciting.

It is time to put down our scripts of suffering, victimisation, unjustified assault and condemnation and see 'life' as it is. Then we are free.

Sickness As a Defense Against the Truth

One of the best-known and most often quoted lessons from *A Course in Miracles* is:

Sickness is a defense against the truth.
(Workbook, p. 257)

I have faced two health challenges recently, one minor and transitory, the other potentially more serious and long term. Because of the latter, I was whisked into hospital for more than two days of tests. Both situations brought this lesson to mind and got me thinking about what truth I was defending against.

Certainly, sickness keeps one's attention on one's body and my experiences were no exception.

The body becomes our almost constant focus at these times, reinforcing the misidentification with who and what we are, which is ceaselessly promoted by the ego even when we're in good health. But sickness intensifies still further the focus on what is untrue, insisting that we are alone, isolated inside this shell of skin, flesh and bone we call our body. This body is a manifestation of our belief in the separation from God. The truth we are defending against is that this idea of separation is a lie.

When the truth gets too close for comfort, the ego needs to distract us and root us in our bodies. Lesson 136, *"Sickness is a defense against the truth"* (Workbook, p. 257), says that we first choose to hide the truth that has been eating away at our illusion of separation by getting ill, then we choose to forget we did it. Thus, it says, our choice is *"doubly shielded by oblivion"*. (Workbook, p. 257)

The ego tells us that sin and guilt are real. In order to escape the spectre of punishment, it projects this sinful, guilty self out of the mind so that it is perceived either in someone else's body (attack) or in our own (sickness). Either way, we forget we made it all up.

Another view is that the misperception of oneself as a body puts a strain on the body that causes sickness. The sickness is not actually in our body, but in the mind that thinks it is a body. Either way, the route to true healing is not by healing your sickness, but by accepting the truth about yourself and letting your mind be healed.

When the ego tempts you to sickness do not ask the Holy Spirit to heal the body, for this would merely be to accept the ego's belief that the body is the proper aim of healing. Ask, rather, that the Holy Spirit teach you the right perception of the body, for perception alone can be distorted.
(Text, pp. 157–8)

True healing is the withdrawal of projections from the body. Then the body becomes an instrument for healing the world, by reminding us that the mind is the source of pain *and* joy.

Now is the body healed, because the source of sickness has been opened to relief. And you will recognize you practiced well by this: The body should not feel at all... there will be no sense of feeling ill or feeling well, of pain or pleasure. No response at all is in the mind to what the body does. Its usefulness remains and nothing more.
(Workbook, pp. 259–60)

During my stay in hospital, I experienced extraordinary care and love – from the hospital staff (even the cleaners) and from my friends, with touching messages of support and concern or impromptu visits, complete with chocolates and grapes. I spent much of the first day fully receiving love and in tears of gratitude. I experienced trust that I was in sure hands. I felt Spirit's tenderness and love, leaving me feeling full, free and connected to God. My job now is to carry that experience of truth – love, connection and wholeness – into the rest of my life.

The Christian Construct

When I first looked at *A Course in Miracles*, I was put off by its Christian language. I had never related to the doctrines of Christianity, so I was shocked to see that this Course, which I had heard so much about, appeared to derive from a Christian belief system.

Of course, I soon learned that ACIM uses familiar Christian terms in very non-traditional ways. Once I understood that, it was as if hundreds of light bulbs lit up in my mind. I began to feel as if I was learning what Christianity was *really* about.

The words *God, Holy Spirit, Christ, Heaven, crucifixion, atonement* and *salvation* are particularly difficult for many people. Once, a participant in a class of mine strongly objected to the word "God" and asked if we could use a substitute. I gently suggested to him that "God" was a perfectly good word so we would continue to use it, but that we would look at what this word meant to him and the reason he had such an issue with it. Likewise, many women have a problem with the Course's use of masculine language: God as a *He* or our *Father*; humankind as *Sons* or *Brothers* and so on. Why is it that words can sometimes be obstacles to understanding? And how do we overcome our resistance to certain words?

A Course in Miracles says that *"words are but symbols of symbols"* (Manual, p. 53) and that things have only the meanings we give them. When you consider it, a word can mean whatever you want it to mean. The word *bonnet*, for example, means something totally different on either side of the Atlantic Ocean. A word is just a string of letters (symbols), with no inherent meaning unless we give it one. Our resistance to some words, then, is just a self-imposed limitation.

If we go through the Course and change the word *God* to something more acceptable to us, or change *He* to *She* and *Father* to *Mother*, we are avoiding and reinforcing the issue that these words bring up for us, rather than dealing with it.

I always explain that the Course comes from the Western Judeo-Christian tradition, which has traditionally used the masculine terminology and, of course, despite appearances, does not exclude women. Once we realise that God doesn't have any genitals, so cannot be a male, and that *He* is just two letters of the alphabet, we can begin to let go of our objections to all these words. In other words, we can forgive them for failing to express the limitlessness of a totally abstract God, Who is neither masculine nor feminine. This is what we can do with any words we object to. In the same way that we deal with anything that pushes our buttons, we forgive them.

Holy Spirit means nothing more or less than the term *Higher Mind*, used in other traditions and philosophies. *Holy* means *whole* and *spirit* translates as *mind*; so *Holy Spirit* translates to *whole mind*. *Salvation* can be translated as *awakening* or even the *enlightenment* of Eastern religions. The *Christ* mind is no different from the *Buddha* mind.

Once we forgive the shortcomings of language and understand the metaphorical messages of the Course, we are well on the way to unlocking its meaning.

One Problem, One Solution

According to *A Course in Miracles*, we have only one problem: We believe we have separated from God and find ourselves in a dangerous, unforgiving world of bodies, space and time. For this one problem there is only one solution and that is to re-experience our true connection with God, which has never been broken.

In this world, we think we have many problems and need so many things. In the course of daily life – eating, maintaining our health, earning a living, etc – there is always something we think we need to do, some predicament to sort out, a thorny problem to solve, or something we need to achieve, gain, improve or resolve.

If we go deeply into each of these problems, asking what we *really* want as a final outcome, we will eventually get to the 'bottom line'. What we really want to reconnect with is the peace and love of God. This is the single solution to our one problem; we're just in the habit of not recognising it.

We put all the *"toys and trinkets of the world"* (Workbook, p. 423) before that one solution, providing the ego's almost perfect smokescreen to keep us blind and seek answers where there are none, certainly none that will ever satisfy the much deeper – almost unconscious – longing for what we mistakenly believe we lost. Each time we ask for these "toys and trinkets", we perpetuate the lie and stay blind to the higher truth.

Gary Renard talks about true prayer, as discussed in the *Song of Prayer* pamphlet, and offers an exercise to experience this. It is set out on pages 351–2 of his book *The Disappearance of the Universe*:

> *The secret of true prayer is to forget the things you think you need. To ask for the specific is much the same as to look on sin and then forgive it. Also in the same way, in prayer you overlook your specific*

needs as you see them, and let them go into God's Hands. There they become your gifts to Him, for they tell Him that you would have no gods before Him; no love but His.
(Song of Prayer, p. 2)

With your eyes closed, visualise yourself approaching God, moving toward a bright white light. Picture an altar in front of you. In your mind's eye, place all the things you think you need and want on the altar as gifts to God. Include all your problems, goals and idols, and leave them there. By giving them to Him you are saying that you put nothing between you and your true relationship with Him. Then, spend the rest of your prayer time in celebration and gratitude for your unbroken connection with Him. Thank God for His Love, for creating you and taking care of you. Forget everything else and get lost in love. Join with Him in true communion.

I have been practising this exercise with remarkable results. The difference between the days on which I do this and the days I don't is clear in terms of my peace of mind, happiness, inspiration and connection with purpose.

It is not that we can't have some of the things we place on God's altar. The *Song of Prayer* says that answers to our seeming problems may come later, in the form of inspiration or guidance from the Holy Spirit – kind of a side effect of communion with God. The real prayer is the song of communion – the "Song of Prayer". The "answers" we receive are the echoes of God's Love.

The form of the answer, if given by God, will suit your need as you see it. This is merely an echo of the reply of His Voice. The real sound is always a song of thanksgiving and of love... You cannot, then, ask for the echo. It is the song that is the gift. Along with it comes the overtones, the harmonics, the echoes, but these are secondary.
(Song of Prayer, p. 2)

Doing or Undoing?

Is *A Course in Miracles* a book about love? At the beginning of the Text, the Introduction says:

> *The course does not aim at teaching the meaning of love, for that is beyond what can be taught. It does aim, however, at removing the blocks to the awareness of love's presence, which is your natural inheritance.*
>
> (Text, p. 1)

I remember taking part in a discussion about whether the Course is about how to be loving, or about undoing the blocks to having a loving experience; in other words, about "doing" or "undoing". The discussion went this way and that with no consensus reached. One participant reminded us that love is what we *are* and presented many passages from the Course that speak about being expressions of love. While I did not disagree with these statements, I think they have to be seen in the overall context of the Course's teachings. For every statement of that sort, I could find one with a different focus.

So, how is this conundrum resolved? To me, it is summed up in those two sentences from the Introduction. We are reminded that love is our *natural inheritance* to remind us of our ultimate direction. Then the focus shifts to the work of the Course: undoing the blocks (our thoughts, beliefs and fears) which we have built to prevent the experience of love.

We find ourselves in this world because we chose against love in the first place, by mistakenly believing we could be separate from God. Since then, the ego has built many defences against love in the guise of being our friend and protector while, all the time, defending against its own demise.

What are these blocks and defences? They are every unloving

thought, judgement, attack, fear, pain, issue, negative belief, shame, drama, or depression. And facing all those is where the work of the Course is. As Course teacher Anna Powell says, "This is not a course in love and light, but one that holds up a mirror to your unflattering side, invites your skeletons to come screaming out of the cupboard."

Yes, love *is* what we are. Intellectually we know that. If it were really as easy as saying, "Only love is real and the rest is illusion," then we would not need 365 lessons, 1,500 pages and an individualised curriculum in the form of our daily life. Repeating that "only love is real" is, as Marianne Williamson puts it, "pouring pink paint" over what is calling out to be healed. The Course does not say: "You are love, so don't bother with the ego." It has page after page of quite graphic descriptions of the ego and its manoeuvres, just so that we can see what we typically do and then choose something different.

The work of the Course is the *undoing* of blocks, *not* a dismissal of them as illusions. It doesn't suggest that we just *be* love and somehow jump to a state of Oneness. We are asked to forgive our illusions, not ignore or deny them. The Course actively warns us against denial, which would only keep the blocks in place and give them more power. ("This is too big and too nasty for me to look at," etc.)

We do not want to look at the darker parts of ourselves and would rather look at light and love, simply *because* we think the ego is real. What other reason would there be? Only the ego itself would urge us *not* to face our blocks, because by not looking at them we keep the ego intact. If we did look, we would eventually recognise the ego as nothing, and it would be gone. So it is the ego who says, "Look only at the light", not the Holy Spirit. He knows no reason not to look and transform the darkness, because He knows it is not true.

The way to remove the blocks is to acknowledge them, look at them, ask for the Holy Spirit's help to see them for what they are

("Help me to see this differently", etc), forgive, correct and undo them.

Thus, we don't have to learn to be more loving or get more love, because love is unchangeable and has never gone anywhere. It is we who have blocked it, by choosing the ego. When the blocks are removed we just experience love; it naturally flows through us and opens our hearts.

Imagine a garden surrounded by a high wall. It is a sunny day, but the wall casts a shadow and keeps the garden in shade. It would be no good, in our darkened garden, to be saying: "The sun is shining. We're in the light!" We would be simply denying that we are in the shade. Once we acknowledge the wall and begin to demolish it, brick by brick, then light can flood into the garden.

Addictions and Specialness

Most of us feel that we *need* certain things in life, whether it's a cup of coffee that gives us a kick-start in the morning, a quick cigarette in the parking lot, a 'fix' of our drug of choice or even that certain person we cannot live without. With these needs, we exhibit an addictive or obsessive pattern of thinking.

I was unaware of this addictive, obsessive part of my mind for a long time, even though I had been told about it often enough. To one degree or another, I have been running this pattern all my life. I can see the craziness, the need for a 'fix'.

My particular addiction takes the form of attempting to obtain validation, approval and love from other people, especially certain individuals. Obsessing about a person is the special love relationship, of which *A Course in Miracles* speaks volumes. However wonderful a person may be, no one can be the be-all-and-end-all, the bee's knees, or the sole provider of everything you think you need. No one is able to fill the gaping emptiness you feel within – only God can! Thinking that another person can provide all this is a massive burden to place on any mere mortal – with feet of clay. That is why no one will ever fulfil all the demands of special love; everyone must fail. No human can fully satisfy us when we are actually seeking what only God can provide – yet we keep looking. That is addiction. As the Course reminds us, the ego's motto is *"Seek but do not find"* (Text, p. 342; Workbook, p. 121; and Manual, p. 34).

Once, a certain person appeared to offer me everything I had always longed for in life: feelings of connection, aliveness, wholeness, passion, completion. Yet I came to realise that these feelings actually had nothing to do with anyone in human form; I really wanted a connection with God to fill the void. I was projecting my yearning for connection with God on to a mere human!

When the relationship changed form, I realised that the pain and emptiness I felt was what I'd been using the other person to avoid. That is, I'd used the relationship to hide from myself. I wanted things to be a certain way so I would feel okay. The break-up gave me the opportunity to look at this and heal it. And I was grateful for that. I used this insight to remember my relationship with God, to feel my completion and wholeness.

I thought I knew about these relationship ideas. However, it is one thing knowing the theory, quite another 'getting' that I'm actually doing it – right now! I think the Holy Spirit said: "You think you've got this stuff? Take this!" It was something I just couldn't avoid. I had to look at my patterns.

If I look to anyone else or anything to give me what I believe I need, I will never receive it and always be disappointed. First, I am affirming my lack by believing that I need anything at all. Secondly, if I look to the form of the relationship – the behaviour and attempt to measure love by the number of phone calls I get, or how timely my special friend is – then I will never receive my real need, which is simply love. Only if I see that the *essence* of any relationship is the Love of God, will I be able to receive fully.

The only way out of addiction or obsession is within the "vertical" or timeless relationship with God, rather than the "horizontal", time-bound connection to the world of individuals. I came to realise that I had never actually desired God to the same extent that I'd wanted things and people in the world. If I could desire connection with God with the same intensity, I'd have it cracked.

As frequently as I could remember, whenever I found myself longing for this special person, I replaced thoughts of my friend with those of God and desired intimacy with Him to the same extent and with the same intensity and passion.

Want and *desire*, which imply lack, are probably not the right words to use about God. In fact, I already have an inherently whole and complete relationship with Him, which merely requires recognition. In recognising that eternal relationship, I will realise that I already have it all.

I certainly struggled to let go of my attachment to the form of my relationship being the way I wanted. Yet, what a gift I was given in letting go! My friend had been my saviour, not in the way my ego wanted, but in the sense that *A Course in Miracles* means it, returning my awareness to the presence of the Love of God.

Relationships Deepening Spirit

We are encouraged to apply the principles of *A Course in Miracles* to our relationships – not merely to maintain and heal the relationships themselves but, ultimately, for their real purpose: to let them be used by the Holy Spirit for the healing of our minds, the transformation of perception, and the remembrance of truth.

We are all in relationship, one way or another – with spouses or romantic partners, children, work colleagues and friends. In the eyes of the Holy Spirit the purpose of all relationships is the same. "And let there be no purpose in friendship save the deepening of the spirit" – from *The Prophet* by Kahlil Gibran.

It is very simple, though usually not easy, to transform a relationship from an unhealthy, codependent one to a healing one – or from *special* to *holy* in Course terms. It is a question of the purpose chosen for the relationship. Is it to keep both people separate, or to join and heal them? Is it to make the ego more comfortable, or to transcend ego?

We think we have to purify ourselves before we can have a healthy relationship, but the opposite is true: a healthy relationship *is* the purifier. The healthy, holy relationship is a tool, and a classroom, for healing.

So long as we believe we are in bodies we will form special relationships. *A Course in Miracles* says that all relationships begin as special ones. We are encouraged to forgive ourselves for our belief in the body and for thinking that we need anything from the other person. This allows our relationships to be used for another purpose.

The simplest level of teaching appears to be quite superficial. It consists of what seem to be very casual encounters... These are not chance encounters. Each of them has the potential for becoming a teaching-learning situation... Even at the level of the most casual encounter, it is possible for two people to lose sight of separate interests, if only for a moment...

The second level of teaching is a more sustained relationship, in which, for a time, two people enter into a fairly intense teaching-learning situation and then appear to separate...

The third level of teaching occurs in relationships which, once they are formed, are lifelong... with unlimited opportunities for learning. [They] *are generally few, because their existence implies that those involved have reached a stage simultaneously in which the teaching-learning balance is actually perfect. This does not mean that they necessarily recognize this; in fact, they generally do not. They may even be quite hostile to each... and perhaps for life.* (Manual, pp. 7–8)

All of these can be healing, holy relationships if we choose a different purpose for them than the purpose chosen by the ego.

Gratitude Spawns Gratitude

We can be so grateful for gratitude! It is incredibly powerful in its effects, as a way of thinking and as a spiritual practice in itself.

Early in my study and practice of *A Course in Miracles*, I began an internal exercise twice a day, night and morning: I thought of all the things in my life I felt grateful for. At the time, these included my work in the oil industry, believe it or not, and the money and opportunities it brought. That included opportunities to travel and to live comfortably, but also my family and friends, companionship, the warmth of the sun and fresh air, nature, country walks, good food, glasses of wine, films, cosy nights in watching TV. My list included non-material things, too: love, loyalty, humour, spirit, God.

The most miraculous thing about this practice was that the more I did it, the more things I found to be grateful for. It was like exercising a mental muscle. It was not easy at first, and exercising engendered some resistance, but the more I used and stretched this muscle, the more powerful it became and easier to use. I believe this practice accelerated my spiritual progress immensely.

For some reason I let this practice lapse and have resumed it, years later.

But why practise gratitude? French educator Jean Baptiste Massieu said: "Gratitude is the memory of the heart." Life coach Charles Burke eloquently observed: "Success is a skill. Happiness is a skill. Gratitude is a skill. Like all skills they must be practised clumsily before they can be done naturally. So if you'll devote ten honest days to the practice of feeling true gratitude and happiness, I can promise you a dazzling new skill. A skill that just naturally attracts success like a magnet draws iron. Because nothing attracts good fortune and success like a joyous, grateful heart."

ACIM talks, similarly, about giving and receiving being one

(Workbook, pp. 195–6). When we give love we feel loved; the more we emanate a sense of fullness with love, the more is given back to us.

This is particularly true in our relationships.

Through your gratitude you come to know your brother, and one moment of real recognition makes everyone your brother because each of them is of your Father.
(Text, p. 69)

Gratefulness may seem difficult in hard times or when problems seem to be mounting up. But gratitude is a very expansive practice. The more we do it, the more we become aware of things to be grateful for – things hitherto taken for granted, or completely out of our awareness. Expressions of gratitude reflect the truth of our inheritance. My perception of my problems has healed considerably since I resumed my gratitude exercise.

[God] *does not need your appreciation, but you do. You cannot love what you do not appreciate, for fear makes appreciation impossible.*
(Text, p. 95)

I've also learned that gratitude is a precursor to abundance. Gratitude allows things to be received and, when we truly receive, we make way for the experience of power and fullness.

With an ever-expanding feeling of gratitude comes a sense of abundance that goes far beyond material things and things of this world. Our minds become ever more aligned with spirit and with the remembrance of the Truth of who we are: complete, whole, perfect and abundant Children of a Loving God.

Today we learn to think of gratitude in place of anger, malice and revenge. We have been given everything… Gratitude becomes the single thought we substitute for these insane perceptions. God has

cared for us, and calls us Son. Can there be more than this?
(Workbook, p. 373)

Can there be more than this, indeed?

The Trade-Off

Have you noticed how elusive perfection is? When we seek and find an improvement in one area, don't we always seem to lose ground somewhere else? In this world, there always seems to be a trade-off. Let me offer some trivial examples of what I mean.

A few years ago saw the demise of London's famous Routemaster buses. Besides being old, the Routemasters were expensive to run, requiring both a driver and conductor. So they were gradually replaced by cheaper buses with a single operator. Although money was saved, the new buses were slower (as they took longer at stops, waiting for passengers to pay on entry) and it was not so easy to get on and off. So, what did they come up with? The so-called "bendy buses" with more doors and, hence, faster entry and exit. Unfortunately, the new trade-off was that these buses were twice the length, causing congestion, blocked road junctions and increased damage to other vehicles.

When I bought my current home, I got a flat in the city, sacrificing space and a garden for convenience and prestige. Now I long for an outside area, but do not want to leave this location. That's my latest trade-off.

Do we not often do this in relationships, too? The ego tells us *"another can be found"* (Workbook, p. 327) if the current one does not make the grade. So, we find someone who does not snore (for example), but get someone who plays loud rock music (or whatever) instead! Why is there always a trade-off? How come we win some and lose some? Why can't we win all the time?

By its very nature, this is an imperfect world because it was made from an imperfect thought: that we could be separate from God, the very essence of perfection. The Son of God erroneously thought that he could wander off and make a home away from Home, where perfection would be thrown away in favour of... shopping!

The world arose to hide [the erroneous idea of separation], *and became the screen on which it was projected and drawn between you and the truth… Do you really think it strange that a world in which everything is backwards and upside down arose from this projection of error? It was inevitable.*
(Text, p. 373)

So what is the answer? Accept the world as it is, and forgive it for being that way. Forgive the imperfection. Then, everything here becomes "perfect" for learning peace of mind and true perfection.

[Teachers of God] *are not perfect, or they would not be here. Yet it is their mission to become perfect here, and so they teach perfection over and over, in many, many ways, until they have learned it.*
(Manual, p. 2)

Here, where the laws of God do not prevail in perfect form, can he yet do one perfect thing [to forgive] *and make one perfect choice.*
(Text, p. 530)

Whatever the circumstances, perfection can be experienced when this change of mind has occurred. No trade-off can impinge upon our peace of mind and on our experience of being in the perfect place at the perfect time, unless we give it the power to do so. In this way, we awaken to the true perfection of ourselves and our perfect Oneness with God.

Forgiveness literally transforms vision, and lets you see the real world reaching quietly and gently across chaos, removing all illusions that had twisted your perception… The smallest leaf becomes a thing of wonder, and a blade of grass a sign of God's perfection.
(Text, p. 354)

You cannot know your own perfection until you have honored all

those who were created like you.
(Text, p. 128)

In the meantime, I would like to write more on this subject but I need to leave room for the next section – another trade-off.

Understanding to Experience

Can there be any point in having a mere intellectual understanding of *A Course in Miracles*, without having an *experience* of what the Course is offering? Can we tell solely by our intellect that what the Course says is true?

I was contacted once by someone who had been a long-time student of the Course (a 'fan', even). He informed me that he had recently rejected the Course as totally "invalid and bogus" and had become a Christian.

I don't have an issue with people rejecting the Course; it happens all the time. The Course is clearly not everyone's path, nor is it intended to be so. Neither do I have a problem with people turning to Christianity or any other path. I know that all paths lead to God, in the end. Everyone needs to choose one that suits their needs and their style.

But this newly-converted Christian posed an intellectual challenge to the Course: "How can you prove what it says is true?"

He declared that he had realised, after many years, that he had been "duped" and "lied to" by the Course, that it was "false, a foul and poisonous deception", "a profoundly dangerous enemy", and even "demonic or satanic, rather than divine in origin". He then set out his rationale for his case. This may seem quite laughable and extreme, but this person is not unique in applying a rational and intellectual analysis to the teachings.

I have to admit that the absolute certainty he had expressed caused me to question my own stance. While I know that many have studied the same Course and have been impressed by its intellectual integrity, consistency and clarity, I am reminded that Chuck Spezzano likens the word 'analyse' to 'anal lies'.

I know that rationally dissecting *any* philosophy can lead to rejecting it. As with statistics, one can make anything prove anything. The ego, the Course says, decides what it wants to be true and then only sees any evidence that supports its view, rejecting anything that goes against it.

Everyone convinces you of what you want to perceive... Everything you perceive is a witness to the thought system you want to be true.
(Text, p. 207)

Perception seems to teach you what you see. Yet it but witnesses to what you taught. It is the outward picture of a wish; an image that you wanted to be true.
(Text, p. 516)

While I am not decrying the value of the intellect, my own experience of the truth of the Course's teachings goes beyond perception and beyond question. No one can shake my complete allegiance to this book, because I have had the *experience* of which it speaks. I *know* forgiveness works, because I experience the inner peace that results from it. I *know* the power of the Course to transform, because I have experienced profound inner changes myself. I *know* the truth of my True Self, because it resonates within me. I *know* my One-ness with God, because I feel the presence of it. I *know* the value of real prayer, as set out in the Course, and experience it on a daily basis. I don't need to believe, or to have faith, because I *know*. This is the shift from perception to knowledge.

All terms are potentially controversial, and those who seek controversy will find it. Yet those who seek clarification will find it as well. They must, however, be willing to overlook controversy, recognizing that it is a defense against truth in the form of a delaying maneuver. Theological considerations as such are necessarily controversial, since they depend on belief and can therefore be accepted or rejected. A universal theology is impossible, but a universal experience is not

only possible but necessary. It is this experience toward which the course is directed. Here alone consistency becomes possible because here alone uncertainty ends... Seek only this, and do not let theology delay you.
(Manual, p. 77)

Many Courses in One

We might think that since we are all studying the same book, students of *A Course in Miracles* would share a fairly consistent idea of what the Course is about and what its purpose is. Surprisingly, this does not seem to be the case. How come? And what is the Course really teaching? Mixing in a wide variety of Course circles as I do, I have come across a wide array of ideas.

To many of us, the Course's principles are meant to be applied to the challenges that life throws at us: from personal crises to problematic relationships and dysfunctional families, in order to transform them. The Course tells us many reassuring things that could be applied to these challenges to help us see them differently. For others, the Course is about living a more guided life, following the Holy Spirit.

To still others, the Course's ideas are used to get what they want, in terms of abundance. They decide what they want to have happen, to achieve or obtain and look for lessons that might help bring that about: "I deserve more money because I am the Holy Son of God." Or it might be about romance: "My holy relationship partner is out there somewhere. The Course can help me overcome my blocks to finding them."

To others, the Course is about how to be happier, more contented, peaceful, or about achieving our full potential. It is about overcoming negative beliefs that cause despondency or depression. It is about healing their issues.

While there is nothing wrong with any of these objectives, I think this focus is missing the point. The Course certainly does offer all this, yet it offers so much more: a path leading to awakening from the dream of separation.

The Course says: *"... the Son of God ask[s] not too much, but far too little."* (Text, p. 556) We ask for more money, better relationships, or greater peace of mind, when all the glory and Love of

Heaven is ours to awaken to!

> [God] *wills His Son have everything. And this He guaranteed when He created him as everything. It is impossible that anything be lost, if what you have is what you are. This... is not understood apart from Him, and therefore has no meaning in this world.*
> (Text, p. 556)

The problem with going for lesser gifts is that they delay us. The ego is the belief that the separation is real and has real effects. In other words, it is the ego that believes we are here and that we have needs. The Course is not about making the ego more comfortable, because that just keeps us stuck in the illusion. Why would we desire to awaken if life here is, at least, bearable? If we focus on what we believe we need or want, here in the world, it makes the world more real to us. And we are not looking at the real problem – the belief in the separation.

Most of us probably realise that the Course is not about fixing the world. But neither is it about fixing *us* in the world, either.

The vehicle the Course offers us, as the means of travelling this path, is forgiveness. Forgiveness does not attempt to offer the ego comfort. Instead it *undoes* the ego, step by step. In the process, some lesser gifts may be manifested, but they are the side effects rather than the focus of our spiritual practice.

Where is Death?

There is, I suppose, a handful of defining moments in life. The death of a parent is one such event.

My father passed away one morning in September 2002, three days before his 81st birthday. His death certificate stated "metastatic lung carcinoma" as the cause of death. Having been told by the doctors that he still had weeks to live, the end came unexpectedly. No one but a nurse was present when, in her words, he "went to sleep."

> *Such is each life; a seeming interval from birth to death and on to life again.*
> (Text, p. 552)

Two hours later, pulling back the curtain, with my mother's arm in mine, to see his body lying in the same bed I had seen him in the previous Sunday, was one of the hardest things I have ever had to do. I felt haunted afterwards by the image of his taut, frozen and waxen face. I kept having the fleeting thought: "There is this thing lying there, but where is Dad? When is he going to turn up?" It took time to sink in.

> *All things but death are seen to be unsure... But death is counted on. For it will come with certain footsteps when the time has come for its arrival. It will never fail to take all life as hostage to itself.*
> (Workbook, p. 309)

I could not believe he had gone – that he was not going to answer the phone when I called, ever again, or that he would not *ever* be there on a Saturday afternoon watching the football results. That part did not seem real – even though the presence of his gold watch on my wrist is a constant reminder that he is no longer here. I cried over every message of condolence I received. In many ways, the pain was beautiful. And, for once in my life, I did not resist it.

I felt grateful that I was able to feel complete with my father at the end. I gave a fairly impromptu eulogy at his cremation. Many were moved as I shared my memories about the kind of man he was, about my childhood and my gratitude to him. My mum and brother were crying in the front row. It was hard, but I am so glad I did that. It was a big step for me.

I miss my dad, yet the brief time of his illness and his death was a period rich in experience. And I feel stronger for it, blessed in many ways. There were many gifts, miracles and lessons learned.

I learned about the true nature of bodies, and life and death. The instant I saw my dad's corpse lying in that bed, I knew without a shadow of a doubt that he was not there. This 'thing' was not him; he was gone. Knowing the theory that we are not our bodies is one thing, experiencing the undeniable truth of that, for the first time for me, was quite another.

The body no more dies than it can feel. It does nothing. Of itself it is neither corruptible nor incorruptible. It is nothing.
(Text, p. 418)

Birth was not the beginning, and death is not the end.
(Manual, p. 61)

I learned about the importance of completing with people and of gratitude. My dad was not the perfect father. Yet rather than focus on what he could have done differently or better, what seems to be the only thing that matters now is the love, support and care I received from him. These are the things for which I feel grateful and for which I was able to thank him in the last six months of his life. Only the love is real.

Of course, it is never too late to forgive, heal and complete a relationship. And I encourage everyone to do this important work.

The Prince of Peace was born to re-establish the condition of love by teaching that communication remains unbroken even if the body is destroyed, provided that you see not the body as the necessary means of communication... communication, which must be of the mind, cannot be sacrificed.
(Text, p. 328)

Let me not see it [the body] *as a sign of sin and death, nor use it for destruction. Teach me how **not** to make of it an obstacle to peace, but let You use it for me, to facilitate its coming.*
(Text, p. 419)

And I learned about allowing, rather than resisting, emotion. In my grieving, I allowed the pain to be, the tears to flow. I knew this was a natural process. Normally, when I feel pain, I see it as a problem that needs fixing. I have learned that it is *resisting* pain that brings suffering, not the pain itself.

Finally, a friend of mine summed it up when he said: "I, too, wonder where we go. Where can we be when we're not here? It's so odd. If only we could fax them. But I think we can... heart to heart. My dad died when I was thirteen. But I still fax him."

Creating Angels with Forgiveness

My father was no angel, but he is now! We had a difficult relationship at times, and I often felt distant from him, unsupported and judged. Born in 1921, he was deeply conservative and undemonstrative, like many men of his generation. So he found it hard to show love and affection. On my parents' 40th wedding anniversary in 1990, he stood rigid as a statue when I hugged him. I decided, in that moment, never again to subject him to such an embarrassment!

He was traditional in the way he thought life should be lived and he judged those who did not see things the same way. It was always difficult for him to understand why I did not continue to follow the career path he had mapped out for me. For years after I began the Miracle Network, he would ask me when I was going to get a "proper job". Our areas of conversation were the safe ones: politics (particularly his suspicion of Europe and admiration of former Prime Minister Margaret Thatcher), work, the house and garden.

At the point of his death in September 2002, suddenly none of this mattered. Over the years, I had begun to have more appreciation of my father's particular way of showing love. I began to see it in the way he had made me a train set, built my brother and me a treehouse in the garden (the best on the street!), and helped us make sandcastles on the beach in Devon. The more I recalled these gifts, the less I remembered his stiffness and distance.

I read the cards of condolence my mother received that week. Naturally, people only write nice things on these occasions, but there were some common themes that stood out – his kindness, his humour and, above all, his conduct as a gentleman. Those appreciations began to take the place of my judgements.

As Marianne Williamson said to me once, it is easy to forgive someone who has died. Maybe it's because he or she is not around to annoy you – or maybe because death helps you see only what really mattered, only what was real. As *A Course in Miracles* tells us, only the love is real.

I finally forgave my father. Though I still remember how I once felt, I now feel only love and gratitude for him, what he gave and for who he was. The rest is gone. Though it would have been wonderful to have reached this point while he was still alive, it is never too late to undo the past. As Chuck Spezzano says: "It is never too late to have a happy childhood."

Miracles are both beginnings and endings, and so they alter the temporal order. They are always affirmations of rebirth, which seem to go back but really go forward. They undo the past in the present, and thus release the future.
(Text, p. 4)

The past can be undone in the present moment, at any time. Why delay and withhold forgiveness from anyone for a moment longer? We will need to forgive everyone and everything at some point – not because the Course says so, but because that is the only way we can truly be free and awaken to our reality and wholeness. So, why not now? What are we waiting for?

When the Ego Won't Let Go

You know the feeling: You've worked on a particular negative thought pattern or a long-standing emotional issue, healed and forgiven it, and you move on. Then, later, when you least expect it, the issue rears its ugly head once more, seemingly just the same. This can be most dispiriting. The ego will attempt to convince you that you have failed (or, worse, that you *are* a failure) and that forgiveness does not work. Perhaps it's meant for others, but not you, so you'd better throw *A Course in Miracles* away and try simply to accept your unhappy lot in life. Does this sound familiar?

The ego is merely a mistaken belief in separation from God. Its goal is to keep us in guilt. By *guilt* I mean all the negative feelings, thoughts and beliefs we hold about ourselves – self-hatred, incompetence, failure, emptiness, unworthiness, lack, incompletion, you name it. The ego wants us to feel guilt because, this way, the idea of separation is kept real in our minds. The ego's rationale is: if we feel guilty, we must have sinned (ultimately, against God) and, therefore, we must be separate from God. Thus, the ego's job is to maintain and compound our guilt.

Guilt makes you blind, for while you see one spot of guilt within you, you will not see the light.
(Text, p. 262)

When the insane thought that we could be separate from God, our Source, crept into our mind and we *"remembered not to laugh"* (Text, p. 586) – that is, when we took the idea seriously – this thought was experienced as this world of separation, duality, time, space and bodies. It appeared to us as if we had destroyed Heaven and killed God!

"How could part of God detach itself without believing it is

attacking Him?" (Text, p. 84) The guilt that came from taking this idea seriously was immense and overwhelming – so much so that it was denied and buried deeply in our unconscious minds.

I have never met anyone who is consciously aware of the delusory belief that they killed God and of the resultant guilt and fear of punishment by God, but the *effects* of it are felt by everyone here. We would not be here at all if we did not have an ego, with its thought system of sin, guilt and fear.

I liken guilt to an iceberg, with only a small part of its reality visible above the surface of the water. The vast bulk of the ice is hidden beneath the surface. The small part we can see is supported and held in place because of the buoyancy of the mass of ice beneath. In a similar way, what we are aware of as guilt in our everyday lives is merely the tip of an iceberg supported by the deep core of guilt about our "sin" against God.

Although the ego needs to keep us in guilt to maintain itself, *"tolerance for pain... is not without limit"* (Text, p. 22). At some point we make a decision to begin listening to the Holy Spirit and start the process of undoing our identification with the ego. We begin chipping away at the iceberg.

What happens as each piece of the iceberg is removed? Due to buoyancy, part of what was hidden beneath the surface pops up into view. So it appears that the iceberg is the same size, that nothing has changed. The good news is that it has got smaller, despite appearances. *"Release from guilt is the ego's whole undoing"* (Text, p. 261).

Next time you appear to be facing, once again, an issue you thought had been dealt with long ago remember that this is a not reason to give up, to think that healing has not worked, or to increase your sense of guilt. Know that it is merely another piece of the iceberg and an opportunity to knock off yet another lump of guilt and to get nearer to undoing the core.

Defying the Laws of Our Nature

I have written about how much we are attached to our ego-concept, yet how tempting it is to skip steps on our spiritual path and deny this attachment, or try to "leapfrog" to spiritual truths without doing the work required to *experience* those truths. We seldom realise that, although we have learned we are not our egos or bodies and the world is not real, the hard truth is that we have bought into the illusion hook, line and sinker.

How many of us would willingly drink a bottle of arsenic, for example? How many of us believe so little in the reality of the physical world that we can defy the forces of gravity and levitate around the room? (If any reader can, please get in touch!) There may be rare, Eastern mystics who can perform such feats, but the rest of us believe in the 'reality' of the illusion so much that the poison would kill us – and we are mostly too attached to our bodies to want that – and we will stay firmly rooted to the ground however many times we recite: *"I am not a body. I am free."* (Workbook, pp. 382–3)

The Course says that *"Illusions are as strong in their effect as is the truth."* (Workbook, p. 242) We know arsenic will kill us – and it will. Yet among some Course students, I have heard scant regard being paid to physical symptoms in the body that could indicate serious illness because "it's an illusion" or "I'm praying about it." I have seen considerable distress being caused by illness while the sufferer refuses to go to the doctor. I knew someone who died of AIDS, refusing any medication for exactly these reasons.

I believe that this attitude is at best mistaken and at worst dangerous. So long as we believe that arsenic will do us harm, fresh air does us good and an aspirin will fix a headache, we would do best to seek professional advice for our symptoms.

The Course actually says that while we still believe in magic –

as all of us who breathe air still do – that the Holy Spirit would rather we take a pill or undergo surgery if that will help to reduce our fear (Text, p. 24). And fear is a major obstacle to spiritual advancement!

Am I saying that the Course is of little practical use to us? Am I painting a depressing and negative picture? No. I believe that it is best that we are fully aware of our real condition, not in denial of where we are and what is so.

While we hold spiritual truths in our minds as the context for our existence and the goal of our healing path, the path of the Course is to work, step by step, on our daily lessons (both in the Workbook and in our relationships).

Eventually – when we have completed this work and have genuinely undone our attachment to and belief in the ego – *then* we will be able to drink the poison and defy the laws of nature.

Until then, most of us have much work to do. When we reach our goal, we will have no use for medicine, doctors, the air we breathe or, for that matter, *A Course in Miracles*.

Crash and Learn

Have you seen the movie *Crash* – not the one by David Cronenberg (1996) about people who get their kicks by crashing cars, but the 2004 film of the same name about the tensions and conflicts of life in Los Angeles? If not, I highly recommend it.

I have been impressed and moved by this outstanding film. As well as having a great soundtrack, it has a deep message for us. On the face of it, this is the staple fare of Hollywood: robbery and murder committed by violent thugs and corrupt police and politicians, egged on by racial and class bigotry. As the movie unfolds, it becomes clear that it is about something else – forgiveness.

It was interesting for me to watch my judgement of the characters, such as the policeman, played by Matt Dillon, who molests and humiliates a beautiful African-American woman (Thandie Newton). His actions seemed beyond the pale of decency; how could he have any redeeming features? Later, though, we see what he is dealing with in his private life – an elderly father at home suffering from a urinary tract infection that keeps them both up at night, in physical and emotional pain, respectively, while struggling to get medical care. Later still, Dillon's character is seen risking his life to rescue the same African-American woman from a burning car on the highway, seconds before it explodes. Then we see what he is really made of.

All the characters in the film are shown to have two sides. There is the ruthless TV director (Terrence Howard) who empathises with a carjacker attempting to steal his 4x4, and the tyrannical socialite (Sandra Bullock), who has no friends in the world, save her maid whom she regularly abuses. At one point she says: "I'm angry *all* the time... and I don't know why."

The belief in separation leads to isolation, alienation, conflict, fear and loss. *Crash* illustrates how bigotry and racial prejudice result in loss and suffering for the perpetrator as well as the victim. It surprised me when I began to understand and have compassion for the abusers. I forgave them readily, as I realised what can make someone fearful and racist. I found myself going from outrage and anger to softening and forgiveness.

The message for me was that these scenes depict the characters' *"call for love"* (Text, pp. 294–6), as *A Course in Miracles* would say. Once you see beyond appearances, beyond the sometimes obnoxious ways people can present themselves, the call for love is clear.

While this does not excuse certain behaviours, it does offer an explanation. How could they not be forgiven?

> *... to give a brother what he really wants is to offer it unto yourself, for your Father wills you to know your brother as yourself. Answer his call for love, and yours is answered. Healing is the Love of Christ for His Father and for Himself.*
> (Text, p. 218)

The film offers a reminder that we are all one. We are all dealing with being human. We all believe we are separate from God and from our brothers (really, our only problem). We are all dealing with the results: fear, guilt and attack. We all deserve to be given a break for believing in this terrifying dream we have made. We are all innocent.

> *How can you manifest the Christ in you except to look on holiness and see Him there?... Behold the body, and you will believe that you are there. And every body that you look upon reminds you of yourself; your sinfulness, your evil and, above all, your death. And would you not despise the one who tells you this, and seek his death instead? The message and the messenger are one. And you must see your brother as yourself. Framed in his body you will see your*

sinfulness, wherein you stand condemned. Set in his holiness, the Christ in him proclaims Himself as you.
(Text, p. 519)

Innocents or Sinners?

It was as a child, made to attend Sunday school and church, when I first heard the concept that human beings are sinners, all essentially bad. The idea that we all had to confess our sins and bow down in front of an angry, vengeful God to ask for mercy seemed to be at the core of religious teaching. And I wasn't even a Catholic!

As a result of this terrifying thought, I took a long hard look at myself and, I'm pleased to say, came to the conclusion that they had got it wrong – at least in my case! All I could see was that I was basically a good person. This was not arrogance, just a deep feeling that I was essentially innocent. Whatever they told me, nothing was going to convince me otherwise. Furthermore, when I considered other people – even serious criminals and those society regarded as being beyond the pale, like Hitler or Myra Hindley – all I could see was that they were sick, unhappy, deluded, or insane but not bad or essentially evil. Over the years, I lost touch with those and many other simple childhood notions; that is, until *A Course in Miracles* reminded me of many of them. The Course has a lot to say about our innocence. It is a huge understatement to say that I have found it deeply reassuring to be reconnected with these ideas.

The Course tells us that nothing we have ever done by identifying with our egos has changed our essential nature one iota. Our true identity remains as it always was and always will be: the radiant, pure and innocent essence of love, at one with the Father, our Creator. However much we may have hidden it, our Christ-Self remains unchanged within us. There is nothing we have to do by way of self-improvement or personal growth to get back what we have lost, because it never was lost, simply forgotten, obscured by clouds of guilt and denial. All we have to do is to remove those obstacles and awaken to what has never changed. We are all the one Son of God; we are as we were created. Nothing God created can be changed by anything we have done. It is actually arrogant of us to think that we could alter what He created. We can never change or reduce our true nature, but we can forget and deny it.

My Self is holy beyond all the thoughts of holiness of which I now conceive. Its shimmering and perfect purity is far more brilliant than is any light that I have ever looked upon. Its love is limitless, with an intensity that holds all things within it, in the calm of quiet certainty... How far beyond this world my Self must be, and yet how near to me and close to God!
(Workbook, p. 420)

Forget not, then, that idols must keep hidden what you are, not from the Mind of God, but from your own. The star still shines; the sky has never changed. But you, the holy Son of God Himself, are unaware of your reality.
(Text, p. 633)

God knows nothing of our illusions. He knows only what He created. We must not wait for Him to get us out of this mess. He waits for us. He gave us free will, the ability to choose. The Holy Spirit will never interfere with our free will and force us. The choice is ours. We choose, in every moment, denial or recognition of the truth that has never changed.

The Course says that it cannot teach us what is already ours, but aims at the removal of the blocks to the *awareness* of what is already ours. All that remains for us to do is to recognise our inherent magnitude and grandeur. If all we see is our littleness that is not because this is the truth about us, but only because we have chosen to delay the "holy instant" when we awaken to the truth.

You dwell not here, but in eternity. You travel but in dreams, while safe at home.
(Text, p. 257)

Thank God I Am Not Special

It is easy to fall into the trap of spiritual specialness when studying *A Course in Miracles*. I should know; I've done it many times. Indeed, I have spent years in a state of spiritual arrogance.

For me, finding *A Course in Miracles* in 1992 was a homecoming. I found a spiritual path that appeared to confirm what I had always felt in my heart to be true. The Course spoke to me like nothing else I had found.

Perhaps it was only natural, then, that I should fall into the trap of thinking that this course was special. If it was my path, it had to be the *best* path. If the Course worked for me then, surely, it would work for everybody, I thought – if only they knew. I found myself comparing and contrasting the Course with everything. Few philosophies met with my approval because few agreed with the Course. Most paths I pooh-poohed, because they contradicted ACIM.

Now I see that every path has its own virtues, and no path is any better or worse than another. I think the Course is great because it is a fast-track course, but that does not make it superior. At the beginning of my ACIM classes, I am careful to state that my intention is not to compare and contrast the Course with other paths. Making comparisons and trying to get the Course to "fit" with another path does a disservice to both.

This is not a course in philosophical speculation... It is concerned only with Atonement, or the correction of perception... those who seek controversy will find it. Yet those who seek clarification will find it as well. They must, however, be willing to overlook controversy, recognizing that it is a defense against truth in the form of a delaying maneuver. Theological considerations as such are necessarily controversial, since they depend on belief and can therefore be accepted or rejected. A universal theology is impossible, but a

universal experience is not only possible but necessary... Here alone
consistency becomes possible because here alone uncertainty ends.
(Manual, p. 77)

The Course itself says that it is only one of thousands of paths
that lead to God. The goal of each path is the same and each is
sure to reach that destination. Each individual will find the path
that suits them and each will travel at their own pace. Fast tracks
are not for everybody and that does not diminish the value of
other ways.

There is a course for every teacher of God. The form of the course
varies greatly. So do the particular teaching aids involved. But the
content of the course never changes. Its central theme is always,
'God's Son is guiltless, and in his innocence is his salvation'... This
is a manual for a special curriculum, intended for teachers of a
special form of the universal course. There are many thousands of
other forms, all with the same outcome... There was never a
question of outcome, for what can change the Will of God?
(Manual, p. 3)

Spiritual specialness is an insidious kind of specialness due to
the very fact that it appears to be "spiritual". Like any other kind
of specialness, however, it results in increasing our sense of
isolation, our separation from others and, however subtly, our
feelings of guilt for having judged a brother.

Spiritual specialness can take many forms, but it always
involves some form of attack, overt or covert. Be honest, do you
like to tell everyone how wonderful the Course is? Do you, like
me, find a variety of ways of criticising or ridiculing another
person's beliefs? Even amongst other Course students, do you
sometimes feel that you have a better, deeper, or truer understanding?

Ask yourself: Do these attitudes stem from a burning desire to share good news, or to convert someone to your way of thinking? Is it really a need to be right? Is your tendency to point out the potential pitfalls of another's way a genuine desire to help, or a need to feel superior or more advanced? If so, is it possible that this need comes not from a wish to contribute, but from a need to sure-up your own doubts and self-doubts?

Does this sort of strategy ever work? Does it not always result in increasing your guilt, that is, your own self-attack? Needless to say, as always, I am not advocating judging yourself if you catch yourself indulging in spiritual specialness; I am simply encouraging you to remember that there are 'horses for Courses'!

A Pain-Free Life?

When we have been on the spiritual path for some years, done innumerable workshops and perhaps completed the workbook of *A Course in Miracles*, we may think that life should be better and, ideally, free of pain. When we have healed whole chunks of the past, and dealt with our parents and primary relationships, the temptation is to give ourselves a hard time when we find ourselves in pain: "Oh no, not this again," we think. Or, "I thought I'd dealt with this last year." We hope that the path is suddenly going to get easier when we begin studying the Course and wonder why it often seems that it has not.

A Course in Miracles says that we only have one problem: the false idea that we have separated from God. A false idea, but nevertheless an idea in which we strongly believe.

It is this thought, the Course says, which is the cause of all our pain. The false idea that we have sinned – originally against God – but also the general idea that we are no good, or even downright bad, leads to feelings of guilt and the belief in punishment, resulting in fear, attack and guilt again. Round and round we go, through this most vicious of cycles.

You can be certain of this: if you believe you awoke this morning and are now reading this book, which you do, you *do* believe in the separation. So long as we are here in this life, on this planet (or any other) and in this existence defined by space and time, we will be making this same mistake. Thus, the cause of our pain remains.

The Buddha said that birth is suffering, life is suffering and death is suffering. This might appear to be a depressing thought, but it is actually a liberating statement. Because we know what egos do, we don't have to worry about them getting better. Your ego is not going to get better. It is beyond hope! You can relax on that score.

What we have to do instead is ask the Holy Spirit to heal our perception of every painful situation, *not* expect Him never to let painful situations arise in our lives.

Before we can choose peace and love, we have to acknowledge that we are experiencing something other than peace and love. For as long as we live here and, therefore, believe in the separation, we will believe in the idea of pain, and will experience pain. Giving ourselves a hard time about that is the same old game of guilt. Just recognise that you are playing the age-old game and decide instead to follow the Holy Spirit's way of forgiveness.

The Course says:

When your mood tells you that you have chosen wrongly, and this is so whenever you are not joyous, then **know this need not be**.
(Text, p. 63)

Although this need not be, we must not beat ourselves up when it *is* so. It is the double bind of feeling bad *because* we are feeling bad that leads us into depression and away from God's Kingdom. Know that you can choose not to feel bad, but know that it's alright that you *are* feeling bad. There is nothing worse than feeling sorry for yourself. Feeling sad, for example, is natural for egos, but the guilt of feeling sorry for yourself because you are feeling sad is the final 'nail in the coffin'. The answer is simply the prayer: *I am feeling bad, but I am willing not to be.*

The question is not about where we really are, but where we believe we are. Theoretically, we know that there has been no separation: *"I am as God created me"* (Workbook, p. 199), but we feel separate because we have chosen to believe in separation. We have to acknowledge that state before we can ask for sanity to be restored to us.

Remember that we have a choice at every step along the way. We have chosen to be here and not in Heaven, and we can always choose to return.

Remember that you are deprived of nothing except by your own de-cisions, and then decide otherwise… You can be as vigilant against the ego's dictates as for them.
(Text, p. 63)

Do not expect knowledge of this to take your pain away, but it will help to get the experience of your pain into perspective. You are doing that stuff again simply because that is what egos do! That is the ego's function, every bit as much as the Holy Spirit's function is to transform your perception of it.

Do not expect to be in bliss all the time just because you study ACIM. It seems to me that the expectation of a perfectly painless life is essentially denial. *"God's Will for me is perfect happiness"* (Workbook, p. 182), but there is no guarantee that we will *be* happy in every moment. Often we choose not to be; but it is still our choice.

Uncomfortably Good News

What constantly amazes me about *A Course in Miracles* is realising, time after time, that it is saying something completely different from what I think it has been saying. Usually, it reveals to me an idea that is not found elsewhere. Curiously, though, it's an idea that I seem to have known before, at some point in the distant past. My respect for this book grows as a result. These revelations, like bolts from the blue, usually leave me reeling: "So *that's* it. That's the truth. Of course!"

The Course is good news, but it is not all 'sweetness and light'. It is not a comfortable ride. I heard someone once describe it as a "destructive book". He was right. What he meant was that it aims at the destruction of who you think you are, every belief you hold, every self-concept and every thought you've entertained about what the world is for. In the end, the message is the most uplifting one that I can imagine, but some foundations of our belief system have to be demolished before the temple of inner peace can be rebuilt. This is challenging. It is a fearful prospect for us and it brings up great resistance, but really there is nothing to fear.

One of my revelations was realising that the aim of the Course is to help us awaken from the dream of separation from God, rather than help us to live better *within* the dream. Certainly a happy dream is preferable to a nightmare but, nevertheless, it is still a dream. Rather than concentrating on improving the dream, we should remember that it *is* a dream and that there is nothing really going on here. If we concentrate on what is essentially valueless, the things of this world, we will miss the true value that lies beyond it all.

The objective is to see our lives for what they are: classrooms for our learning. We do not have to make the circumstances of our lives (the dream) better, only learn and grow from whatever circumstances present themselves. In this way, we learn to tread lightly in this world, knowing that we are not in danger and that our goal is secure.

Any work we do that uses ACIM to improve our situation – for example, to develop better relationships or become more prosperous – is fine and definitely not wrong. Anything that reduces fear is desirable, but ultimately, our personal circumstances are simply tools for awakening. The Course says that our destiny *is* to awaken and that we can only delay that inevitability with our absorption in the world of things. Looking at the reason we might want to delay that destiny points us to the root of the problem.

Joining hands, singing songs and hugging each other at workshops or conferences mean nothing. Of themselves, these behaviours do not represent real joining. Like anything, their value lies in what they are used for. They can be gateways for joining, but they can also be, as Marianne Williamson says, like "pouring pink paint" over our pain. They can provide emotional highs that make us feel good for a while; temporary relief of our symptoms, but not a cure for the disease.

It's vital that we look at the cause of our problems: our false belief in separation and the fear that this has generated, embodied by the ego. Looking at this is not a fashionable thing to do, I know. It is considered "negative" to look at our darkness. It is certainly negative to *dwell* on the darkness, but we do need to look at it to dispel it. Pretending that it is not there only "makes the error real", reinforcing our belief in it. When we look at the dynamics of the ego dispassionately with the Holy Spirit's help, we will see its insanity – the fact that all our pain is based on illusion. If we can gently laugh at the ego, it will cease to maintain its fearful hold on us. Of course, this is the last thing that the ego wants us to do and that's why we are so resistant to doing it. The ego would rather have us learn how to be more creative, or develop our psychic powers and so on. With such techniques, we reinforce the dream and thus the ego's domain is never threatened.

Take off the covers and look at what you are afraid of. Only the antic-ipation will frighten you, for the reality of nothingness cannot be frightening.
(Text, p. 219)

... the deeper you go into the blackness of the ego's foundation, the closer you come to the Love that is hidden there... Do not leave any spot of pain hidden from His Light, and search your mind carefully for any thoughts you may fear to uncover. For He will heal every little thought you have kept to hurt you and cleanse it of its littleness, restoring it to the magnitude of God.
(Text, p. 243)

Our sense of autonomy – that is, our specialness that we spend our lives nurturing, the thought of having a will separate from the Will of All – is illusory, but that's where the ego wants us to focus our attention. This obsession with our "little selves", always trying to make them feel better within their dream, limits our attention to our bodies. This blocks the mind's extension and reinforces the feeling of separation, the cause of all our perceived problems in the first place.

We need not be afraid to look at this situation, our fear and our darkness. And it is necessary that we do so in order to see it for what it is: an insane joke and a denial of our true Identity. I believe that we are being called to look at what the ego is doing, not simply to ignore it and convince ourselves that life is wonderful all the time. It will not be an easy path, but I believe it is what the Course is encouraging us to do. And it is this that really excites me: Truth. The time for delay is over. Let's get serious with this!

Your 'guilty secret' is nothing, and if you will but bring it to the light, the Light will dispel it. And then no dark cloud will remain between you and the remembrance of your Father.
(Text, p. 241)

... the more you look at fear the less you see it, and the clearer what it conceals becomes.
(Text, p. 287)

Transcending Anger

To a large degree, anger is taboo in polite society. We British, especially, are often taught that we should not show anger, so the emotion is suppressed. As we grow up it is common for anger to be denied. If we attend self-development courses, we may learn that it is good and healthy to express anger. Then it becomes a matter of believing that we owe it to ourselves to express how we feel every time our "buttons are pressed".

A Course in Miracles has a very different take on anger, teaching that neither its suppression nor expression is of value. Instead, the Course teaches us how to let it go.

ACIM says that *"anger is **never** justified"* (Text, p. 638), but what does that mean? Does it mean that we should not feel angry or that we should not express anger when we feel it? Not at all. The Course always cautions against denying our bodily experiences and this includes our feelings, whether positive or negative. We all feel angry at one time or another and there is no use denying that. What *"anger is **never** justified"* means is that it is a mistake to attempt to validate or justify our anger.

It is often said that to express anger is "empowering" and that we should honour our feelings. Unfortunately, the truth is that anger is profoundly disempowering and dishonouring of ourselves.

Whilst the suppression of anger can lead to illness (self-attack) and its expression can thus be regarded as a healthier option, continued venting does not actually move you toward the healing of your anger.

One may be tempted to feel that if enough anger is released, someday there will be none left. But the situation is more like a burst water pipe – you can keep emptying buckets full of water for the rest of your life, but until you fix the leak the problem remains. The cause of anger is still there.

Our anger is designed as an attack on others or the world, justifying the projection of guilt and, therefore, justifying a punishment that is seen as "deserved". ("Look what you did. You made me angry, so I am right in seeing you as the guilty one.") The projection of guilt on to another is what egos love to do. The result of making someone guilty in our minds is that *we* then feel guilty for what we know, deep down, to be an unwarranted attack on a brother. And "guiltier" is what the ego wanted us to feel all along; that's the ultimate purpose the anger serves. That is not what the ego will tell you, of course. It will tell you that attack was justified, that another person or the world at large was at fault, so they deserved it. Anger truly is a case of our cutting off our own nose to spite our face. It is, in truth, an attack on ourselves. In short, anger is not wrong; it just does not work.

So, what do we do when we feel anger, as we inevitably will? What would be *A Course in Miracles'* approach? First: feel it. (Expressing it, in some non-destructive way to take the 'charge' off it, may also be a useful thing to do.) Second: as soon as you are able, forgive yourself for it. Third: take responsibility for it. Fourth: express the desire, in prayer, to see the situation differently. Ask to see peace instead of attack. Say: *"I could see peace instead of this."* (Workbook, p. 51)

Feeling guilty about feeling angry – *"I'm not supposed to feel this way. I'm supposed to be spiritual"* – just plays into the ego's hand. Anger is an inevitable part of our human experience. So, accept it – but resolve to let it go, rather than project it as guilt on to another and reinforce it in yourself.

Forgiveness, as always, is the key. Forgiveness is our release from the guilt that was the cause *and* the result of our anger and attack. True forgiveness brings us to the place where we know the innocence of ourselves, our brothers and the world, and where we know the truth of the statement that our *"anger is **never** justified"*.

Hatred Turned to Love

Watching a news item on the latest political agreement in Northern Ireland, between parties at one time violently opposed but seemingly, now, united in a desire for peace, reminded me of my first workshop in Belfast, in February 2006.

My visit to Belfast and Londonderry was a highlight of my teaching experience. The Belfast workshop was held on the campus of the famous Queen's University. In the afternoon of the second day, we looked at the theory and practice of forgiveness. During the break that followed, my friend Claire suggested that we conduct a forgiveness process between the Protestant and Catholic participants.

This turned out to be one of the most powerful exercises I have ever witnessed. We asked those who regarded themselves as coming from the Protestant community of this divided province to stand on one side of the room and those who regarded themselves as Catholic to stand on the other. We invited the two groups to form rows facing each other across the room. The moment this was done, what had hitherto been a restrained group dissolved into floods of tears as the pain of decades and generations of division came to the surface.

Claire and I invited the groups to take one step at a time toward each other. The idea was that they would meet in the middle of the room. In fact, so eager were they to join that the 'sides' needed no encouragement. They were in the centre hugging one another before I knew what had happened. Although the process occurred faster than anticipated, the result was perfect. It was enormously moving to witness and I was so overcome with emotion, myself, that I could barely speak.

This exercise had demonstrated powerfully both the pain of separation and the desire to forgive in this divided society. It was also clear to me that, wherever we live, the pain of our self-imposed isolation is almost intolerable and that our longing for true connection is massive – despite political, social, religious, cultural, racial, ethnic, economic, and class divisions, and despite our deeply cherished and fixed positions, our need to be right, to find fault, to point the finger of blame, and to justify our claims of being unfairly treated.

We all just want to join with our brothers in what is merely the recognition of our true state. Despite what the other may have said or done, or what we think or feel, I believe this is always the case. The pain of denying the truth is just too much to bear.

Let your mind wander not through darkened corridors, away from light's center. You and your brother may choose to lead yourselves astray, but you can be brought together only by the Guide appointed for you. He will surely lead you to where God and His Son await your recognition. They are joined in giving you the gift of oneness, before which all separation vanishes.
(Text, p. 290)

Clearing Writer's Block

When I first found myself as editor of *Miracle Worker* magazine, I wondered how on earth I was going to think of something different to write about for each issue. I was still quite new to *A Course in Miracles*. How could I have anything of interest to say to anyone? I was not even a writer. So I used to panic every two months at the thought of an impending publication date. Yet, something always came in time.

In fact, I have not missed a single issue. Without fail, material has come that I felt inspired to share with readers. It has been an interesting process. So I'd like to share something of my experience of channelling, guidance and creativity.

I have never regarded myself as any kind of channel, but I have realised that, in my writing, channelling is really what I am doing. But I don't regard this as a special talent or ability; in fact I think that everyone can do it.

When the right intention is there, I am able to get out of the way long enough for the truth to shine through to my conscious awareness. In those times of panic, there was no chance that anything to write would come. If I sat down with pen and paper (or finger and keyboard) and tried desperately to think of something to write, to force it, absolutely nothing happened. I got total writer's block.

When I was relaxed, it was just there. Usually the material came quite unexpectedly in times of peace. Sometimes a single thought would inspire me and I was away. Walking or driving have often been times of inspiration. (I understand that the rhythm of walking actually puts one into a kind of light trance.) The problem, while out and about, was that I usually did not have any means of recording what came. If driving, I had to pull to the side of the road and write before the inspiration went away.

At these times, I just know the words to write – whole

sentences forming into paragraphs. It is as if they are simply presented to me, complete. All that is required is a bit of tinkering with details and rearranging of order. In the process, I find associations between ideas of which I had not been aware and things I did not even know I knew.

When I am not trying, I am allowing and there is flow. There is a magical experience of everything coming together as a complete and whole creation. I am now able to trust the process and, in that trust, there is opening.

I still do not know if I am really channelling (I don't ordinarily use that word), or whether I am just inspired, tapping into my creative potential, or even whether there is any difference. Receiving guidance is the same. I hand over my fears and anxieties to the Holy Spirit. In the peace that follows, I know that the guidance is always the same: "It's okay. Everything is perfect. There is nothing you need to do."

I never hear a voice, but I know the words. I 'hear' the words as if they are my own thoughts, but they are not Ian Patrick's thoughts. They are my real thoughts, *the thoughts I think with God"*. (Workbook, p. 83)

Darkness and Light

The 2008 Miracle Network conference was entitled "Being the Light". And, if I am honest, I found it difficult to decide what to speak about. I must admit that I'm much more familiar with what we could call my 'dark side' than of being the Light.

I have called the ego our "default option". Like a computer default, it is the thought system automatically adopted unless another choice is made. When I wake up in the morning, the ego is already engaged and in charge. Thoughts like "Oh no, another day at the computer"; "Oh dear, I have to deal with so-and-so today" or, as Robert Holden jokes, "Good God, morning!" (rather than "Good morning, God"!) indicate that the ego is in charge.

Every time I feel even a twinge of anger, irritation, frustration, dissatisfaction, fear, sadness, loss, envy or guilt; hold a grievance or a judgement; doubt myself; or feel alone, not good enough, unloved and unlovable; different from, less than, or better than others – in short, every time I believe the ego's lies – I am in darkness. This I've experienced all too often.

It is common in spiritual circles to want to deny that we have negative emotions. We do not want to own our dark side; this evasion is sometimes called a "spiritual bypass". We do not want to deal with uncomfortable things, but jump over them and be happy. We think that's what it means to be spiritual. However, I do not think that is the path of *A Course in Miracles*.

[Darkness] *cannot be evaded, set aside, denied, disguised, seen somewhere else, called by another name, or hidden by deceit of any kind, if it would be escaped. It must be seen exactly as it is, where it is thought to be... For only then are its defenses lifted, and the truth can shine upon it as it disappears.*
(Workbook, p. 469)

We have to see our darkness for what it is, without any disguise, pretence or justification. And this is not easy. The darkness is the ego's defence and keeps it in business. It does not want to let it go. Not looking keeps it in business. Indeed, looking is usually the very last thing I want to do. I will delay, project and assert that I'm right – anything but look at my own 'stuff'. All the while, my ego is kicking and screaming: "No, don't look. It's not true. It's too awful [see how contradictory the ego is]. Others are to blame anyway." The end result is that the darkness is made real or reinforced.

Loudly the ego tells you not to look inward, for if you do your eyes will light on sin, and God will strike you blind. This you believe, and so you do not look... Beneath your fear to look within because of sin is yet another fear, and one which makes the ego tremble. What if you looked within and saw no sin?
(Text, p. 454)

Fortunately – like the Sixth Cavalry – help is at hand, in the form of the Holy Spirit, to remind us that sin is not real, that we made it all up as a bad dream. Once our dark side has been acknowledged and, with a *"little willingness"* (Text, pp. 380–3) offered to the Holy Spirit for correction, the rest is up to Spirit, who will undo what never was. I know that when I have the courage to do this, it is like waking from that bad dream.

Like the sun obscured by clouds, the Light in us is obscured by clouds of guilt. As they are removed through forgiveness, the Light, which was always there, naturally begins to shine ever brighter. And this becomes our gift to the world.

"To teach is to demonstrate." (Manual, p. 1) With our forgiveness work underway and our Light shining, we demonstrate the way forward for others, simply by being who we are, like a beacon in the darkness.

There are only two thought systems [light and darkness], *and you demonstrate that you believe one or the other is true all the time. From your demonstration others learn, and so do you... Any situation must be to you a chance to teach others what you are, and what they are to you. No more than that, but also never less.*
(Manual, p. 1)

Time for Year's End

What do you think about at each New Year? Is it a time to make resolutions, to wipe the slate clean and start all over again? Is it a time of symbolic rebirth, or just another date on an arbitrary calendar?

Perhaps, to you, the dawn of a new year is just a day like any other. Perhaps you are taking seriously the ACIM assertion that time is just an illusion. So why get excited about an illusion, right? But don't you get excited when your football team wins? Would you not get excited if you were to win the lottery? Do you say: "What football team? What lottery?" Illusions, right?

It might be nice to understand that time is an illusion, but how many of us actually live as if yesterday did not happen? We think that life will be a certain way because of the patterns of the past. *A Course in Miracles* says that we see *only* the past. (Workbook, p. 11) We think that we could be different if only the circumstances of our past had been different.

> *The ego invests heavily in the past, and in the end believes that the past is the only aspect of time that is meaningful... its emphasis on guilt enables it to ensure its continuity by making the future like the past... By the notion of paying for the past in the future, the past becomes the determiner of the future... The present merely reminds [the ego] of past hurts, and it reacts to the present as if it were the past... although the past is over, the ego tries to preserve its image by responding as if it were present.*
> (Text, pp. 245–6)

The past can have no hold over us unless we bring it with us. *A Course in Miracles* offers us a way of letting our past go, through forgiveness. Forgiveness is the very essence of the lesson: *"The past is over. It can touch me not."* (Workbook, p. 442) If we truly forgive, we let go of the past. It is as if it never happened (because it didn't). We exist in the present moment and the future (another illusion) is a clean slate.

The New Year can be seen as a metaphor for letting the past go, dropping old fears, old guilt, old grievances and for stepping forward into a future unencumbered by the weight of the past (memories, pain, beliefs). Every moment in our lives is the perfect opportunity for us to make a new start. A clean, unblemished future awaits us in every moment, ready to have written on it whatever we wish.

Each new moment can symbolise rebirth. Have a great future!

Unless the past is over in my mind, the real world must escape my sight. For I am really looking nowhere; seeing but what is not there. How can I then perceive the world forgiveness offers? This the past was made to hide, for this the world that can be looked on only now. It has no past. For what can be forgiven but the past, and if it is forgiven it is gone.
(Workbook, p. 442)

The Greatest Love of All

Loss features in all our lives at one time or another. The death of a dear friend of thirty years, after a long illness, hit me hard. My friend Lida had always been a fixed point in my life, always there and always supporting me, through thick and thin. We went on several holidays together; she was like a family member. Soon after her passing, another friend decided to cut off from me, for his own reasons. Both people had been prominent in my life and losing them left a big, painful hole.

As human beings, I think we all tend to look outside ourselves for support, for a sense of who we are and for love. It seems a natural thing to do, but it does not actually reflect our truth.

After the sadness and grieving over my losses, I began to see that I was being called upon to refocus, to turn within. I realised this was a lesson in being more self-reliant or, more accurately, Self-reliant. It was about turning to look inside to God, to what is permanent and True. It was not about isolating myself, rejecting company, or saying other people did not matter, but about finding what is really true *within* relationships, rather than focusing on their forms – including the form of the body.

As Whitney Houston's 1980s song, *Greatest Love Of All*, says:

… Because the greatest love of all is happening to me / I found the greatest love of all Inside of me…

The loss I experienced was only on the level of form. In truth, the essence of these relationships could not be destroyed through death or abandonment. When I shift my focus from the world of form to the freedom that is found only in God,

I sacrifice illusions; nothing more. And as illusions go I find the

gifts illusions tried to hide, awaiting me in shining welcome, and in readiness to give God's ancient messages to me... And every dream serves only to conceal the Self which is God's only Son, the likeness of Himself...
(Workbook, p. 462)

While I was looking to the illusion of form, I was denying myself the gifts that were thus hidden from me.

Furthermore, the Course says: *"I was created as the thing I seek."* (Workbook, p. 459) The qualities I thought would be given to me by someone or something outside myself, I had already and would rediscover once I began to look in the right place.

What is it that *"I was created"* as? What are *"the gifts illusions tried to hide"* (Workbook, p. 462)? The Course answers:

The Son of God is limitless. There are no limits on his strength, his peace, his joy, nor any attributes his Father gave in his creation.
(Workbook, p. 460)

Sure enough, I have noticed a profound shift, depending on where my thoughts are at any given time and on what I choose to focus. I can be lonely and in need, or joyful and peaceful. It is purely a matter of my choice. And praying for help in remembering the truth and forgiving my misperceptions is how that choice is made.

Special Relationships

Special relationships seem to be most people's favourite subject! In our culture, special relationships, particularly those of a romantic nature, are regarded as the ultimate prize, the goal for which we seek. Hence the countless popular songs on this subject, all the boy-meets-girl movies and other pop media idealisations of what a relationship should be.

By idealising the special love relationship, we romanticise what the Course exposes as the biggest weapon in the ego's arsenal. The ego, doing what it does best – keeping us in guilt – uses such relationships for its own ends.

The special love relationship is the most devious device because it appears to be something it is not. While the ego tells us it is what we want and need, what will save us and the goal we are seeking, it is, in fact, a smokescreen for fear, attack, blame, guilt and shame.

That is not to say that relationships cannot be genuinely loving, healthy and intimate. The Holy Spirit offers us another way: the holy relationship. It is important, however, to see what the ego is up to before looking at how its works can be transformed.

The ego urges us toward relationship with the idea that we are fundamentally lacking, incomplete and not good enough on our own (what the Course calls "guilty"). Otherwise, why would we be looking for anything or anyone in the first place? We would only be looking if we believed a love relationship would bring us completion.

In Spain, they have a saying that we are like half oranges looking for another half orange to complete us and make a whole orange. We come with needs, looking for someone who can meet those needs and give us what we believe we are lacking – whether that be simply company, or true love and fulfilment.

If we find someone who does meet our needs and we appear to meet theirs, it may seem as if this is a relationship "made in heaven". "This is the one," we might say. "I finally made it." Underneath, however, to keep itself in business, the ego is busily reinforcing our guilt. How?

Fundamentally, using someone to meet our needs is stealing from them. Even if the relationship seems to be "give and take", we will feel mistreated if we get less back than we give out. *"Whoever seems to possess a special self is 'loved' for what can be taken from him."* (Text, p. 342) Many subtle bargains are thus struck in the name of 'love'; often we are "giving to get". (Text, p. 58) This is not love at all, but manipulation and theft. And on some level, we know that and feel guilty for it. The ego rubs its hands in glee.

Not only are we stealing from the other person, we are not seeing them for who they truly are: a child of God. We are seeing them as a body and, worse, are probably focused on certain body parts. Inevitably, certain physical characteristics of the person are most likely to attract our attention. (Personally, physical attraction is very important to me.)

> *Even the body of the other, already a severely limited perception of him, is not the central focus as it is, or in entirety...* [Particular parts become] *centered on and separated off as being the only parts of value.*
> (Text, p. 355)

Seeing someone merely as a body, or a collection of body parts, is actually a subtle attack on them, for which we must inevitably feel guilty. "Another thing to feel guilty about," the ego shouts gladly.

In this world, nothing ever stays the same for long. People change, move on, or grow old. What happens when the other person no longer meets our needs as he or she once did or, worse, finds someone else to love? Our guilt, which had been at least kept in check by romance, begins to surface. We may try to make the other feel guilty and revert to former ways: "What happened to you? You used to love me. You used to do such-and-such for me. Look at you now!" This is what Ken Wapnick called the "Jewish mother syndrome"! And this pressure may work, for a time, if one's partner feels guilty enough to comply. You can see, by now, that this is not love; it's an attack, resulting in more guilt on both sides.

This may seem like a depressing view of romantic love, which we're used to thinking is so beautiful, positive and maybe even spiritual. The difficult truth is that it does not work for very long. And the ego would, of course, have it no other way!

It is vital, if we are to find a better way, to first see "special love" for what it is and be honest about it. The Course says all relationships must begin as special, otherwise we would never form them in the first place. Our function is to turn all of them over to the Holy Spirit to be used for His purposes, not ours. In that light, Marianne Williamson suggests that the first thing we should do, the moment we realise we are falling in love, is pray!

The Holy Spirit's purpose for all relationships is that they be used for healing, forgiveness, and ultimately remembering who we truly are. He will use them, if we ask, to show us that we are already whole oranges! This is the 'holy relationship' – the special relationship transformed. Thus, the ego's greatest weapon can become the Holy Spirit's biggest gift.

Becoming Spiritual

At one time or another, most of us find ourselves wondering if there might be something we could do to be more spiritual: begin a new practice, make an altar, start going to church, lead a more holistic life, *feng shui* our home – any activity which would deliver more spiritual content to our lives. We tend to assume that we have to *do* something in order to be spiritual, but perhaps we're missing the point. Sitting in church, for example, we might actually feel anything *but* spiritual. And this demonstrates that being spiritual is not about doing anything. It is about *being*. It is not what we do. It is really a question of what anything we do is for, how we hold it in our minds, the significance or the purpose we give it. The question to ask ourselves is whether the purpose we have given something in our minds is about love, joining and forgiveness, or about attack, separation and guilt, regardless of appearances or what we may have read in spiritual books.

A Course in Miracles never talks about what we should do, on the level of behaviour, but only about what we think (the purpose we have given to something). Within our illusory world there is no activity that is inherently more spiritual than any other. Nothing has any meaning in and of itself. There is no lifestyle – be it vegetarian, alternative, green, ethical, egalitarian or capitalist – that is more or less spiritual than another. Any of these can be practised with love, or with hatred and judgement. This is another example of the confusion between form and content (purpose).

The same goes for eating only kosher or halal food, or fish on Fridays, being circumcised, wearing feathers of the 'juju' bird on your head to ward off evil spirits, or going to Holy Communion. The belief in spiritualising matter rests on thinking that if you do a special thing you are saved, and if you do not you are a sinner. Neither is true.

Judge nothing by how it appears, but ask yourself only what it is for. Purpose is everything. So, there is nothing we need to do, nor *can* do, to become more spiritual. The essence of our being *is* spirit. Our job is to remember that, regardless of any activity we undertake.

> *Only the purpose that you see in* [anything] *has meaning, and if that is true, its safety rests secure. If not, it has no purpose, and is means for nothing. Whatever is perceived as means for truth shares in its holiness, and rests in light as safely as itself... The test of everything on earth is simply this: "What is it **for?**" The answer makes it what it is for you. It has no meaning of itself, yet you can give reality to it, according to the purpose that you serve.*
> (Text, pp. 515–6)

Pearls in the Poop

A Course in Miracles says that everything that happens to us can be used either by the ego for our crucifixion, or by the Holy Spirit for our salvation. I have often struggled with this idea. I say to myself: "This problem is bad news. I hate this about myself. It is horrible. How can any good come of this?" and so on.

Within every sin – that is, every negative thought or belief that we act out – are positive qualities that psychologist and workshop facilitator Duane O'Kane calls "the pearls in the poop". These are the gifts waiting for us in all our pain and in every trauma. For example, within the emotion of fear is the gift of excitement. Good actors use the energy from stage fright to give a bravura performance. As someone said to me once: "Fear is excitement without the breathing." Likewise, some of the gifts within anger are passion, energy, commitment and focus. People who stuff-down or deny their anger, as I sometimes do, tend to be cut off from these qualities.

> *The Son of God can make no choice the Holy Spirit cannot employ on his behalf, and not against himself. Only in darkness does your specialness appear to be attack. In light, you see it as your special function in the plan to save the Son of God from all attack, and let him understand that he is safe...*
> (Text, p. 530)

We could think of these negative thoughts and beliefs about ourselves as being our "special guilt" – the particular way we seem to be uniquely flawed. The Course refers to the way we act out such beliefs as our "special sins":

> *The special messages the special hear convince them they are different and apart; each in his special sins and 'safe' from love...*

(Text, p. 503)

It calls the gifts waiting to be claimed our "special graces". Our special sins can be 'flipped' to reveal the gifts they hide. For each special sin, we have corresponding special graces.

The specialness he chose to hurt himself did God appoint to be the means for his salvation, from the very instant that the choice was made. His special sin was made his special grace.
(Text, p. 530)

One of the things I do to myself is competing with people close to me, which leads to inevitable feelings of envy and inferiority. I am beginning to see this not as a curse but as a blessing, an opportunity to discover hidden graces. Instead of resisting the experience, thinking that this is a bad situation and trying to get rid of the pain as quickly as possible, I have begun to allow myself to experience envy and inferiority fully, and really get into it. Why? Because all my suffering comes from resisting the pain. In the very midst of the anguish is an experience of God, if I stay open to what is to be found there. This is an opportunity, even though it sometimes feels like death.

I am beginning to see what the pearls in this particular poop are. In the midst of the hurt about not feeling good enough are the gifts I have been throwing away. Right there is someone who is sensitive, deeply caring (of self) and self-loving. In that totally surrendered place is the place of tenderness, compassion and incredible love. I have begun to accept that I am okay. The gifts to be found here are beginning to make my feelings of competition and inadequacy seem inconsequential. I feel that this new sense of myself is the gift here. I am beginning to embrace these aspects of myself. They are quite beautiful and I love myself for them. (Now to love myself regardless!!!)

Yet if the Holy Spirit can commute each sentence that you laid upon yourself into a blessing, then it cannot be a sin.
(Text, p. 531)

I have become aware of two voices in my head and my ability to choose between them. The ego voice is always there, seeking and finding evidence that I am not good enough. It is loudest and seems to speak first, shrieking raucously, but I have been able to "thank it for sharing", then remind myself that what it says is not true and choose not to listen. Instead, I can hear the Voice for Truth telling me that I am good enough just as I am.

Combating Level Confusion

One often hears students of *A Course in Miracles* dealing with something difficult or unpleasant with the comment, "It's just an illusion." You're running late for an important meeting and someone says: "Time is an illusion"; or, perhaps you're having a fight with a partner and fob it off with: "It's not real, anyway."

Occasionally, and much more seriously, someone dismisses the tumour growing inside them as "just an illusion" and does nothing in accord with the principle *"I need do nothing."* (Text, pp. 388–9) Tragically, this has happened on more than one occasion.

I think this kind of talk can give the Course a bad name, but it is a commonly held misunderstanding of the teaching. It's the type of dismissal that the Course is referring to when it says that denial of the body is *"a particularly unworthy form of denial."* (Text, p. 23) Rather than deal with the challenge in front of us, there's a tendency to try not to face it. This is a symptom of what Ken Wapnick identified as "level confusion", that which causes a huge amount of misunderstanding.

Although it never explicitly refers to the idea, the Course is actually written on two conceptual levels. Level I, in Wapnick's system, contrasts the Reality and Truth of the Oneness of Heaven with the illusory nature of the physical world of time, space and bodies. Level II, on the other hand, is the practical level of dealing with the world on a day-to-day basis. It is the level dealing with the split mind, which contrasts the wrong mind of the ego with the right mind of the Holy Spirit.

While Level I is the metaphysical truth, providing the foundation of the Course's thought system, Level II is where we need to do our work with our relationships, feelings and bodies, giving them over to the Holy Spirit for the purpose of healing. Level II is where our lessons of forgiveness are learned (or not).

Although the Course is written on these two levels, it tends to switch readily between the two without warning or any indication that it is doing so. It often switches levels in the same paragraph, possibly even within a sentence!

Two examples follow.

You are the dreamer of the world of dreams... Nothing more fearful than an idle dream has terrified God's Son...
[Level I]

So fearful is the dream, so seeming real, he could not waken to reality... unless a gentler dream preceded his awaking... in which his suffering was healed and where his brother was his friend.
[Level II]
(Text, p. 584)

Speaking of God's Plan, which exists in His Mind:

It is apart from time in that its Source is timeless. [Level I]

Yet it operates in time, because of your belief that time is real.
[Level II]
(Workbook, p. 177)

Once I grasped the concept of levels in the Course, the truth of it became clearly apparent and made the book much easier to follow. In fact, without keeping this idea in mind, the Course can be confusing and appear to contradict itself. Once I got the idea that there is no contradiction between the two levels, that they are both true at the same time, I wondered why I had not seen it before.

So, now we can see how to resolve the apparent contradiction of dealing with situations facing us in a world that we are told is not real. We have to see them clearly on both levels: the practical and the metaphysical. We do the inner work of finding peace and healing, for example through prayer and forgiveness, *and* we deal with whatever we need to deal with, in practical terms, whether it means going to the doctor or marriage guidance.

A friend of mine who required an organ transplant approached his family about the possibility of one of them becoming a donor. No doubt as a result of their fear and guilt, they replied that he should be praying more and asking God for help. No! He needed to put his trust in God and pray for peace and resolution, *and* find someone to give him an organ.

Next time you have some complex and challenging project underway and someone says: "Just trust in God," it does not mean that you can stay in bed all day and do nothing while the work somehow gets done by a superior being. It means that you do what you need to do to get organised and ready to act according to your guidance, *and* trust in God. As the saying goes: "Trust in God and tether your camel."

The Ladder of Prayer

The Song of Prayer, a pamphlet that derived from the same source as *A Course in Miracles*, talks about the "Ladder of Prayer".

The lowest level of prayer attempts to use God like Father Christmas; in other words, you're giving Him your shopping list. Although this might be a beginner's level of prayer, it is preferable to seeing yourself as a helpless victim of circumstance who has no resources to call upon. The catch is that the ego tells you the things you are asking for will bring you what you really want – happiness – but unfortunately they won't.

Praying for such things may indeed bring them into being. To some degree, prayer works in that way; we are all able to psychically manifest *something*. No doubt you've noticed that some people seem to be able to draw money to themselves or find parking places with ease. This should come as no surprise and there's nothing wrong with it, but seeking happiness outside yourself doesn't work. Getting what you want in the world of time and space does not deliver lasting peace, despite all the ego's protestations to the contrary and its continual search to prove that it does.

The highest form of prayer is not even asking for help in resolving situations in the world, whether they be personal or global in nature. Asking for things to go a certain way is like saying that you know better than the Holy Spirit about how things should be, and it is still looking outside yourself for resolution. What is nearer the mark is asking Him to restore you to your Right Mind; in other words, helping you be at peace in the given circumstances, whatever they may be.

Never attempt to overlook your guilt before you ask the Holy Spirit's help. That is His function. Your part is only to offer Him a little willingness to let Him remove all fear and hatred, and to be forgiven.
(Text, p. 383)

Even prayers for helping other people are only mid-range on the ladder. The Course says that such a prayer is, in fact, an attack on others, because we are seeing them as less than God created them. Only the arrogance of the ego would have you think that there is something in you that they lack and that can be restored by your prayer. This may be difficult to accept as, once again, this radical thought system proves itself to be exactly the opposite to the way the world thinks.

Going one step up the ladder, a prayer for your own peace of mind is more to the point, but it confirms that you do not already possess such peace. So, better still is a prayer of gratitude for all God's gifts. These are not physical gifts, though. The "gift" is *you* and all that you are. As an extension of God, God's Son shares His Father's characteristics, all of which can be described as Love. Thus God gave us everything at our creation. There is no need to ask for what we already have.

That means that your natural state is one of abundance. I do not necessarily mean material abundance, but that is not excluded. After all, there is no reason why you should not make your dream as materially abundant as you would like. But what earthly gifts can compare with the gifts of God?

Recognising my God-given gifts quickly restores me to my Right Mind, but the "Ladder of Prayer" goes higher still.

The only meaningful prayer is for forgiveness, because those who have been forgiven have everything. Once forgiveness has been accepted, prayer in the usual sense becomes utterly meaningless. The prayer for forgiveness is nothing more than a request that you may be able to recognise what you already have.
(Text, p. 45)

If you regard a prayer as being sent by you to another entity, i.e. the Holy Spirit, then it is dualistic and therefore reinforces the idea of separation. The Holy Spirit is not outside you but, ultimately, the only thing that will save you is help from *outside the ego's thought system*. This help is always available, but it needs to be invited because the Holy Spirit always respects your free will.

The Holy Spirit, the Voice for God, is always there, because He is within our own minds. What is always present cannot be lost. Therefore, He cannot fail to hear you and cannot fail to answer. He is always calling, but you may fail to listen or take any notice. My own feeling is that His eternal answer to me is always simply, "It's okay. Just relax."

The Course says that the highest level of prayer is the song of Love between the Father and the Son – the way it was before the separation seemed to happen.

Prayer is the greatest gift with which God blessed His Son at his creation. It was then what it is to become; the single voice Creator and creation share; the song the Son sings to the Father, Who returns the thanks it offers Him unto the Son. Endless the harmony, and endless, too, the joyous concord of love they give forever to each other... The love they share is what all prayer will be throughout eternity...
(Song of Prayer, p. 1)

Stop It, I Like It...

I like to call a spade a spade in this book. This chapter is no exception. You think that you want inner peace – but do you? If you really wanted it, surely you would have it.

A Course in Miracles offers a path to inner peace. It gets you there by showing you all the blocks that are in the way of that experience. The Course shows you how to surrender those blocks to the Holy Spirit, who will gently lay them aside until all that is left is the peace that you desire.

The main obstacle to peace, however, is your desire for something other than peace. If you had chosen peace, you would have it. If you are not at peace, it is because you have chosen something else. You *think* you want peace, but if you do not have it, it is because you do *not* want it.

The Course talks about your unconscious attraction to what you fear:

> *No one can die unless he chooses death. What seems to be a fear of death is really its attraction. Guilt, too, is feared and fearful. Yet it could have no hold at all except on those who are attracted to it and seek it out.*
> (Text, p. 416)

It is only by recognising that you have chosen not to be at peace that you can stop and ask yourself if you would care to choose again. If you convince yourself that you want peace when you do not, you are deluding yourself and that's why you are stuck with a lack of peace, i.e., unhappy.

If you are in London and want to be in Edinburgh, you have first to acknowledge that you *are* in London and then start moving northward. You will never get anywhere if you convince yourself that you are already in Edinburgh!

Likewise, if you find that you are not at peace, you do not say: "I want to be peaceful." You obviously do not and you're not really facing the problem. Instead, you can say:

I must have decided wrongly, because I am not at peace. I made the decision myself, but I can also decide otherwise. I want to decide otherwise, because I want to be at peace. I do not feel guilty, because the Holy Spirit will undo all the consequences of my wrong decision if I will let Him. I choose to let Him, by allowing Him to decide for God for me.
(Text, p. 90)

We have been given "free will" and the Holy Spirit will not violate that. When your prayers appear to go unanswered, could it be that you are not being honest with yourself about what you really want? The role of forgiveness, in any situation, is to allow you to see through the illusions and delusions that you have placed in the way of peace. Forgiveness literally *undoes the world*. Along the way it unties the cords that bind you to your pain, guilt and fears.

Before you can forgive, you must acknowledge that you condemn. If you pretend that all your thoughts about the world are full of light, you are deluding yourself. The Course says: *"The ego is… capable of suspiciousness at best and viciousness at worst."* (Text, p. 176) I know mine is. Isn't yours?

The guilt you will feel when you look at the viciousness of your ego thoughts is a common experience. It is all part of the ego's game of guilt and punishment. Be kind to yourself. Learn to laugh gently at the insanity of the ego.

I am aware that on many occasions I choose not to be peaceful; I would rather be right than happy. And that is fine. A tremendous freedom comes from this kind of honesty. By admitting the truth to yourself, by taking responsibility for your own thoughts, you are no longer at the effect of those thoughts.

You are acknowledging that you are the cause of your own painful feelings. It is only then that you can, with the help of the Holy Spirit, choose again.

From Death to Life

Death is a difficult subject, but one that cannot be avoided forever. We all apparently have to die. It is one thing that we can be certain of, is it not? As a child, I used to wonder: What if I was dead? What if I had never been born? Where would I be then?

The concept we call *death* is, perhaps, the most predominant aspect of the concept we call *life*. *A Course in Miracles* says that this is a world dominated by death. In fact, this is a world of death because it is inseparable from life. From the moment we are born, we are on our way out. To be alive implies that there will be death. In addition, we cannot survive here without the death of other living things, be they people, animals or plants.

I speak of death and life as concepts because that is exactly what I mean. Like everything, they are ideas, and as the Course repeatedly tells us, they are mistaken ones. In truth *"there is no death"* (Text, p. 51) for the sole reason that there is no life (at least, not as we think of it). This world, our lives and our bodies are mistaken beliefs about who we are. This world is not our home; it appears to be real, but it is a collective hallucination. And the good news is: if we were never born, then we can never die!

That does not mean that we can retain our physical bodies forever. Certainly, death is an illusion, but that is not to say that we will not dream about it happening to ourselves and others. We should not use the concept of the illusory nature of death to deny that, within this world of time and space, we will appear to die. Immortality is a fact, but it is not a fact of the body.

A typical Christian perspective asserts that when we die we will automatically, somehow, find ourselves united with God in Heaven. *A Course in Miracles* says that this cannot happen unless the illusion of separation is undone first. Death, while the belief in separation remains, is merely another part of the life/death illusion. After death we will remain separate, albeit without our physical bodies – perhaps to reincarnate – until Atonement has occurred.

"No one can die unless he chooses death" (Text, p. 416), just as no one can live unless he chooses life. The choices are the same and neither is true, in the sense that we usually think of them. The perception of separation – which leads directly to our experience of life and death as real – is a choice we make. In truth, however, *"There is no death"* (Text, p. 51) but it is the same thing as saying: "There is no life."

The preoccupation with overcoming death merely serves to "make the error real" in Course terms, since the mistake is thinking that there is something to overcome. Undoing the illusion of death is no different to undoing any other illusion. Once one of them is gone, all of them will be gone.

You might be wondering what practical use any of this might have, especially in the face of our own death. At the very least, it is comforting to know that whatever may appear to be happening to us, the truth of Who we are remains safe and well, in another "place" altogether: the Self which literally and absolutely never dies. With the Holy Spirit's loving guidance, this understanding can lead to the final undoing of this perceptual realm altogether.

The world is not left by death but by truth, and truth can be known by all those for whom the Kingdom was created, and for whom it waits.
(Text, p. 51)

Giving Miracles

I have puzzled over what *A Course in Miracles* means by "giving" a miracle. "Experiencing" a miracle, yes. "Accepting" one, yes. But offering or giving one? How is that possible?

My difficulty stemmed from the idea that, for me, miracles take place in my mind – with a little assistance from the Holy Spirit, of course. A miracle would be my change of perception, my forgiving someone, or my accepting grace to heal some aspect of my mind. So I wondered: How, then, am I able to give that to another person? As the title of Lesson 345 says, *"I offer only miracles today, for I would have them be returned to me."*

The same lesson goes on to say:

Father, a miracle reflects Your gifts to me, Your Son. And every one I give returns to me, reminding me the law of love is universal... The miracles I give are given back in just the form I need to help me with the problems I perceive.
(Workbook, p. 476)

I wondered if "giving a miracle" might simply mean forgiving another person, as in offering them forgiveness. But the Course pamphlet *A Song of Prayer* says:

As prayer is always for yourself, so is forgiveness always given you. It is impossible to forgive another, for it is only your sins you see in him. You want to see them there, and not in you. That is why forgiveness of another is an illusion.
(Song of Prayer, p. 10)

I just had to get to the bottom of this. What exactly does it mean to be a miracle worker? To find out, I asked several renowned Course teachers* how they understood the concept of "giving a miracle". Their replies had many similarities, but also some differences.

It seems that my giving a miracle *is* more than just something that goes on in my mind. There is something more going on, beyond the oft-quoted line in the Course that *"the sole responsibility of the miracle worker is to accept the Atonement for himself."* (Text, pp. 25–6 and Text, p. 85) Giving a miracle is more than a personal decision to let fear go and let love be. Giving a miracle is more than simply having kind, loving, or appreciative thoughts about someone or performing a kind act.

A miracle is a change in perception. My miracle restores me (temporarily, at least) to my right mind and corrects errors in my thinking. Our first responsibility is to accept healed perception for ourselves. And, in turn, I give that miracle to someone else by extending to them what was given to me.

It is essential... that the miracle worker be in his right mind, however briefly, or he will be unable to re-establish rightmindedness in someone else.
(Text, p. 25)

And that extension will happen naturally. It could mean offering forgiveness; it could mean seeing them as the holy Son of God.

In practice, I may offer others another way of looking at themselves, someone else, a problem or a situation. I may do this verbally, as advice, or by teaching in a classroom, in counselling or psychotherapy. Or I may do it with thoughts or remote healing. Even a smile, a hug, or a touch can remind someone that they are okay. From the Course's point of view, however, it is not the action (the *form*) that does anything but the *content* of it – that is, the thought behind the behaviour – which has power to heal others.

The process that takes place [is] one in which the therapist in his

*heart tells the patient that all his sins have been forgiven him, along
with his own.*
(Psychotherapy, p. 16)

Ultimately, the miracle is forgiveness, the release of a grievance.
With the right intention, I can help another person to do that.
This will show them their innocence as a child of God, their
changeless perfection, help them recognise that we are all
connected and at one with God, or help them perceive a situation
as the Holy Spirit would.

When I forgive someone, the healing in my mind (the miracle
worker) passes to the mind of the other (the miracle receiver)
since all minds are joined, resulting in some form of healing in
their mind, too. As the Workbook says: *"Let peace extend from my
mind to yours, [name]."* (Workbook, p. 147) That, in turn, might
even result in some form of physical healing. In this way, miracles
are beyond that which happens in my mind only – they are
actually interpersonal. My healing is shared with my brothers.

A good example of this is the ability of Jesus, as related in the
Bible, to heal others. Course writer Marianne Williamson
suggests that his perception of himself and the other person was
so healed, and he was so convinced of the wholeness of both, that
the other person was also convinced and was consequently
healed in both mind and body.

Giving a miracle is not about extending helpful behaviour (yet
does not exclude it), but about extending a healed perception.
When I forgive myself, the increase in light in my mind becomes
available to everyone, if they choose to accept it. Giving a miracle
means seeing the other in the light of truth and, perhaps, saying
or doing something that helps them connect with their own right
mind. When I extend the blessing of forgiveness, I experience a
feeling of grace, of true joining. It does feel as if I have given
something (a miracle) from the part of my mind that remembers
my oneness with God and my brothers.

*(With thanks to Nick Davis, Michael Dawson, Nicola and Robert Perry, Miranda Macpherson, Anna Powell, Allen Watson.)

Our Purpose in God's Plan

I often hear the idea that we have a specific life purpose, a plan for our individual lives that has been devised by God, like a mission it is our duty to follow. Such a mission might include being in a specific job, living in a particular location, working with certain people, or doing explicit "good works" in the world.

There are certainly places in *A Course in Miracles* where this is suggested, for example: *"You are indeed essential to God's plan."* (Workbook, p. 180) But, appealing as this idea might be, I do not believe this is what the Course is saying.

We determine our purpose here depending on which part of our minds we choose to identify with at any given time. If we choose the ego, the function of which is to keep us stuck, small, unhappy and trapped in the world without the hope of going home, then that will become our purpose.

If we choose the Holy Spirit, then the purpose of our lives changes to being that of a classroom, in which we heal our misperceptions through forgiveness, and thus remember Love and awaken to our true identity.

Forgiveness is my function as the light of the world.
(Workbook, p. 104)

… my function must be happiness.
(Workbook, p. 110)

My purpose, then, is still to overcome the world. (Text, p. 144)

My function here is to forgive the world for all the errors I have made.
(Workbook, p. 208)

God's plan is simply this: The Son of God is free to save himself, given the Word of God to be his Guide.
(Workbook, p. 225)

When the Course speaks of God's Plan, that is what it means. When it speaks of an individualised curriculum (Manual, p. 70), it is because all our lives are seemingly different. The Answer in all of them, however, is forgiveness, whatever specific situations we are presented with. When the Course says: *"...everything that happens, all events, past, present and to come, are gently planned by One Whose only purpose is your good"* (Workbook, p. 255), that is also what it means. The gentle plan is healing through forgiveness. What else is there to do?

[*"Salvation is my only function here"*] *is the Thought that saves and that forgives, because it lays no faith in what is not created by the only Source it knows. This is the Thought whose function is to save by giving you its function as your own. Salvation is your function, with One to Whom the plan was given. Now are you entrusted with this plan, along with Him.*
(Workbook, pp. 177–8)

Oh, how the ego would love to convince us that God intends us to do specific work here in the world, and sets up specific situations for us. That would make us *very* special, would it not? More importantly, it would also mean that we are really here in a real world, rather than experiencing an outward picturing of an inner condition. The ego's ultimate goal is to keep us believing we are individual bodies living real lives separate from God so that we may forget our divine purpose, which is to awaken to the Truth.

The line *"Remember that no one is where he is by accident, and chance plays no part in God's plan"* (Manual, p. 26) thus takes on a different meaning than is often given it. It means that a new perception is always available to us, whatever the circumstances.

There are no errors, because there is always a lesson to be learned and Truth can always be the result.

In the early years of my Course study, I can see how I was tempted to believe that my own work in setting up and nurturing the Miracle Network was somehow orchestrated "from above". In fact, I think the organisation has been effective because we have mostly remembered our real, inner work. By that means, the way has been eased (even in the most challenging moments).

The peace of God is everything I want. The peace of God is my one goal; the aim of all my living here, the end I seek, my purpose and my function and my life, while I abide where I am not at home. (Workbook, p. 390)

Illusion and Disillusionment

I was shocked and saddened to hear that a friend had killed himself, after several failed suicide attempts. Mark was a member of a spiritual group I attended. Although I had not known him long, I had grown to like him. He had wanted to help me in the office and I greatly appreciated his sense of humour.

It was clear that Mark had a lot of anger and unresolved issues from his past, yet I knew that he had worked through much and achieved some breakthroughs. He knew a lot about Buddhism and had a wide experience of different spiritual paths.

Thus I was puzzled over what had driven him to take such a drastic step. What had led him to the point where he saw no point in living, nothing in the world worth carrying on for, and no hope? I realised that, in one way, he was correct. There *is* no hope in the world outside ourselves.

Marianne Williamson talks about the word *disillusionment*. We say someone is disillusioned when something does not work out; they see no hope for a plan, dream, or relationship and so they give up. The truth is, Marianne says, that it was an illusion in the first place!

In truth, there is nothing in the world outside ourselves that is going to bring us salvation. To many, this will be a depressing idea. Yet there is another way of looking at it, which leads to our ultimate salvation. In truth, all hope lies in turning to God, which is the power of Love within us. That power comes from beyond the physical world of time and space, and not from anything we can see in this world. In that metaphysical source there can be no disillusionment, no disappointment or let-down. It is a solid rock of truth that ultimately leads us home.

The Bible talks about setting the foundations of our house firmly on rock, rather than on sand that can easily be washed away. Looking to an ever-changing and unreliable world for safety, security and meaning is to build on sand. Do we want to build on sand or rock?

Allen Watson has written a wonderful booklet entitled *What is Death?* In it, there is a section on suicide that I found very helpful. It refers to a section in *A Course in Miracles* that seems to talk about suicide:

> *Men have died on seeing this* [that there is no hope of salvation in the world], *because they saw no way except the pathways offered by the world. And learning they led nowhere, lost their hope. And yet this was the time they could have learned their greatest lesson. All must reach this point, and go beyond it.*
> (Text, pp. 653–4)

Could it be that Mark had realised this, yet had made one final, fatal mistake? Had he believed that there *really* was no way out but to take his own life, when seeing the situation differently could have been his greatest breakthrough?

Mourning Mark's passing brought our small group together like nothing else had done before. Yet could Mark's greatest gift be the lesson he can yet teach us, if we allow him to? This lesson brings new meaning to the phrase *"choose once again"* (Text, p. 666): truly give up on the world, as the Course encourages us to do. However, that is not the same as giving up on life. Instead, this can be the point where we begin to live with a new awareness of our ultimate reality.

There is every reason for hope if we look for it where it truly is, instead of seeking for it where it is not.

We Are Never Alone

Have you noticed how so much of our culture is built on the idea of being in a relationship or having a family? This idea is so prevalent that the first question many friends ask is about my relationships: "Hello. How are you? Are you seeing anybody at the moment?" If I answer, "No," I notice a look of sympathy on their faces.

There is a common assumption, even in New Age and spiritual circles, sometimes unspoken, that there is something wrong if one is not in a romantic relationship. So much self-development work is geared to teaching that romantic relationships are the ideal for human beings.

But, if we are honest, the desire for a relationship often comes from a sense of lack, incompletion, scarcity and fear. We feel the need to be with someone, either on an intimate basis or just to 'hang out' with. And we feel lonely when there is literally no *body* around.

The fear of being alone is one of mankind's greatest anxieties. Feelings of loneliness can lead to desperate measures to find anyone to fill that gnawing sense of emptiness inside. Further, I believe that the New Age emphasis on relationships can actually increase our feeling of need and foster a sense of inadequacy if we do not have the kind of relationship that society expects.

I am not suggesting that there is anything wrong with intimate relationships. I am certainly not suggesting you should leave your partner! It is our motivation for having such a relationship that deserves a closer look. Is our motivation a genuine impulse toward partnership, or a need to fix feelings of inadequate self-worth? I particularly encourage looking at the assumption that there is anything wrong with being alone.

The idea that there is anything wrong with being single is based on the misperception of lack, that one is somehow unhealed and missing a vital component. This is what the Course calls the "scarcity principle". It is the foundation of the ego's thinking and the search for special relationships.

The whole teaching of *A Course in Miracles* is that there is no lack, there is nothing wrong; you are innocent, healed and whole already. The only lack is that we have forgotten this happy fact.

The Course also teaches that, in truth, we are not alone and we cannot be alone. We are already in relationship; we cannot *not* be. It does not matter whether we live alone or sleep alone; we are always in some form of relationship. The forms vary: some are with family, others are with friends, acquaintances, colleagues, neighbours, tradesmen, shopkeepers and passers-by. But even without a lover, one cannot help but be in relationship.

A Course in Miracles speaks of the truth of our union with all these people, with everyone else and with creation. In truth, we are in relationship with everyone and with our Creator more intimately than we could ever be in any worldly relationship. All that is missing is our experience of that fact. All that is left for us to do is to experience that natural relationship. *A Course in Miracles* gives us the tools.

Whatever we may believe about ourselves, there is nothing we can do to alter the reality that there is no lack in us, regardless of our life situation.

Making A Difference

At the risk of seeming to have a fixation on death, here I go again! One day last winter, I was walking with some friends along a stretch of the south coast. We passed the ruins of a house, set back from the beach. It had clearly been many years since the dwelling had been inhabited; it was a mere shell. We began to speculate on who might have lived there and on their lives.

I thought about the one-time occupants living, sleeping, working, playing, eating and loving on this spot. They were, no doubt, long since dead. Now, what was left of that energy and of those lives? Essentially, nothing. It occurred to me that for the vast majority of humans, there are no traces – not even memories – left behind of our lives after two or three generations. What difference or lasting effect will any of us have made on this planet, one or two centuries after our deaths? None. All traces of us will have gone, like those of the inhabitants of this house. It will be as if we had never existed. It was a depressing thought.

Then, I realised that there is one lasting difference we *can* make: the way we affect other people. The people whose hearts we touch by extending love, who are changed by our presence in their lives, take that change into their being and go on to touch others in some way. These effects spread like the ripples from a stone thrown into a pond, through space and down through the ages. And time can only magnify the changes.

A Course in Miracles suggests:

A miracle is never lost. It may touch many people you have not even met, and produce undreamed of changes in situations of which you are not even aware.
(Text, p. 6)

Every time we extend an act of forgiveness, kindness,

185

compassion, love or acceptance, we touch another and make our mark. Fearful thinking and attack foster and reinforce separation. An act of kindness, however, reflects our inherent oneness with one another and teaches others who they really are.

The Course says: *"To teach is to demonstrate."* (Manual, p. 1) We are all teaching, all the time, by how we live our lives and thereby what we demonstrate to others. This applies not just to people in formal teaching positions or giving workshops, but to all of us. We are all capable of receiving and thereby offering miracles to others.

A friend of mine shared with me the story of being in a relationship with a man who did not share her enthusiasm for spirituality, particularly *A Course in Miracles*. In fact, he called her beliefs "rubbish" and felt threatened by them. Through gentle and loving encouragement she eventually got him to open up and share his innermost thoughts and feelings. Sometimes, he would resist and revert to attacking and ridiculing her ways. Slowly but surely, though, he began to see the benefits of being honest and open, and working through his resistance to healing.

He began going to counselling and, during one session, the family secret of childhood abuse came out. He began to work on healing that trauma and the mistaken beliefs he had taken on as a result. He told his mother what happened thirty-odd years ago and she, in turn, confronted his father. The secret, the 'elephant in the room', was exposed. It could hardly have been comfortable for them, but the family was presented with a golden opportunity to heal and transform. As I told my friend, the boyfriend and his family were changed forever for the better by her. There can be no going back.

This may be an extreme case. But we can touch people in smaller ways, too, such as by extending loving kindness, or by being a shining light of love, acceptance and forgiveness. Ask yourself: How much difference will you make? What will your legacy be?

Repeating Ourselves

Isn't there something terribly familiar about that *déjà vu* feeling – like you have experienced it sometime before? Do you find yourself repeating the same kind of situations and relationship patterns – you know: different people and different circumstances evoking the same feelings and emotions? Why does that happen, that *Groundhog Day* feeling?

A Course in Miracles says that if we have made a wrong decision about ourselves in the past, we will be presented with opportunities in which the Holy Spirit will urge us to make a better choice until we *do* get it right. Whatever is unhealed in ourselves will be acted out repeatedly in our life circumstances, until our minds are healed of those issues.

Trials are but lessons that you failed to learn presented once again, so where you made a faulty choice before you now can make a better one, and thus escape all pain that what you chose before has brought to you. In every difficulty, all distress, and each perplexity Christ calls to you and gently says, "My brother, choose again."
(Text, pp. 666–7)

It is no surprise, then, that some situations seem horribly familiar. The pitfall is the temptation to use such experiences to confirm that our negative belief is correct, rather than seeing the situation as an opportunity to choose a better way.

Whatever guilt (*"faulty choices"*) we have denied in our own minds will be projected outward on to the world, other people and situations.

What we feel guilty about is reflected back to us in the faces of other people. The guilt we secretly feel, but have buried, will be shown to us by the mirror of the world, particularly by our "shadow figures", those we accuse of acts we think that we would never commit. Accusing others, or the world, keeps us from looking within at our shameful feelings and thus denies the possibility of healing where the error was made – in our minds. Not only that, but our grievances against others actually increase our own feelings of guilt. As Chuck Spezzano says, when you point an accusing finger at someone else, you actually have three fingers pointing back at you.

It is only too tempting to accuse others and to feel that we are the victims of actions or situations beyond our control. Of course, the world will generally support the belief that we can be attacked and that defence is, therefore, both justified and required. And so the world winds wearily on, stuck in the vicious circle of guilt, blame, victimisation, attack and guilt.

My big issues centre on abandonment or rejection, and competition or jealousy. This derives from sibling rivalry born along with my brother, when I was two and a half. It felt as if my mother was rejecting me although, as an adult, I realise she had her hands full with the new arrival. My father was somewhat absent, physically and emotionally. The truth is that I rejected *them* but, rather that own that, I turned it around and felt rejected *by* them.

I have been replaying that scenario over and over again throughout my life. For example, I tend to wonder why people so often let me down. To my mind, unreliability equals rejection. Of course others may not really be unreliable; I just perceive them that way.

A new way of thinking that exactly reverses the way of the world is presented in *A Course in Miracles*. That way is forgiveness. True forgiveness requires taking responsibility for our lives and all the challenges we face. It requires taking back everything we have projected outside our minds on to the world, returning us to the point where the projection took place: our wrong decision about ourselves. In truly looking at the contents of our minds, we are reminded of the truth that also lies there –

our innocence and wholeness, in the eyes of God.

When that innocence and wholeness is our fundamental experience of ourselves, the vicious circle is broken. We can awaken to a brand new day, with no need to repeat *Groundhog Day* – our patterns – because we have taken back our projections from the world.

I am learning to *"choose again"* and thus remember the truth of my wholeness and love-ability whenever I am tempted to indulge in old thought patterns. Gradually, I am experiencing these habits less and less. When they do arise, they seem to trigger less of an automatic reaction in me than before.

He would not leave one source of pain unhealed, nor any image left to veil the truth. He would remove all misery from you whom God created altar unto joy. He would not leave you comfortless, alone in dreams of hell, but would release your mind from everything that hides His face from you.
(Text, pp. 666–7)

Forgiving Is Not "Nice"

In a box on the front page of every issue of *Miracle Worker* magazine, it says: "The state of Heaven, the peace of God, is reached through the practice of forgiveness." Why is this so? And why does forgiveness figure so prominently in the message of *A Course in Miracles*?

The aim of the Course is the attainment of inner peace. Heaven, in this regard, is not a physical place, but rather a state of mind.

I used to think that I should forgive people because I was striving to be a nice person, and that was what nice people did. Although they might have hacked me off, it was "spiritual" to let them off the hook. What this type of forgiveness amounted to was nothing more than a behavioural change – I was being nice towards them, but in my mind I still held them "guilty as charged".

The Course has taught me that, despite what anyone may have done (take any extreme example you care to think of, it makes no difference), if I hold a grievance about it, then it is I who suffers, and I am in hell. *"You condemn only yourself, so do you forgive only yourself."* (Workbook, p. 73) *"Who could be set free while he imprisons anyone?"* (Workbook, p. 366) Forgiveness is not just about releasing the other person from their perceived guilt, it is about releasing myself.

It is one thing to be guilty in the eyes of the law, by the conventions of society, or even by our own homemade standards of personal conduct, but we are all innocent in the eyes of God. God sees only the innocent Son that He created. To release ourselves from our self-made hell of guilt, we must see our brothers as God sees them. If we see them as guilty, we will see the guilt in ourselves and feel terrible. *"To hold a grievance is to forget who you are."* (Workbook, pp. 114–115) When we remember to see as our Father does, then we see the innocence in our brothers and in ourselves; we see the Christ in them and recognise it in ourselves. When we see them as they are in Reality, we see ourselves in Reality.

It is only by remembering who we are in this way that we can recognise our true Selves and thus reach the Kingdom of Heaven, the peace of God, which is our natural state, our true inheritance.

Forgiveness gently looks upon all things unknown in Heaven [and] *sees them disappear.*
(Workbook, p. 365)

Through your forgiveness does the truth about yourself return to your memory. Therefore, in your forgiveness lies your salvation.
(Workbook, p. 104)

Every time we are tempted to attack or condemn anyone for any reason, it is an opportunity to remember who we are, through forgiveness; and not for the other person's sake, but for ours. Thus, the other person has the potential to be our crucifier or our saviour, depending on what we choose to be for them.

How do we forgive? Kenneth Wapnick outlined what he called the "Three Stages of Forgiveness". The first stage requires that we take back the projections we have placed on others and the world, and take responsibility for our own pain. The second stage is having the willingness to change and to recognise that forgiveness is necessary for peace of mind. This requires asking the Holy Spirit to allow your mind to know the truth. In the third stage, the Holy Spirit erases our attack thoughts and undoes the guilt. That is the good news: in the third stage you do not have to do anything. Just allow the Holy Spirit to work on your stubborn mind and it will happen. It's a miracle!

My friend Lynda Bates' inspiring life story has contained

many opportunities for forgiveness. Several years ago, in the space of just a few weeks, due to a single mistake on her part, she lost her husband, her family, her house and her friends, and then got thrown out of her church. Through the practice of forgiveness, though, forgiving herself and those around her, she found peace, regained her self-respect and ultimately found her Self. Finding that forgiveness had so transformed her life, she wanted to share the concept with others. She went on to write a book on forgiveness, conduct a weekly phone-in show on the subject on a radio station in Denver, Colorado, USA, during which she talked people through their issues and taught them how to forgive in any situation. She also had a forgiveness column syndicated in newspapers in the United States and in *Miracle Worker* in the UK.

Therefore, hold no one prisoner. Release instead of bind, for thus are you made free. The way is simple. Every time you feel a stab of anger, realise you hold a sword above your head. And it will fall or be averted as you choose to be condemned or free. Thus does each one who seems to tempt you to be angry represent your saviour from the prison house of death. And so you owe him thanks instead of pain. (Workbook, p. 366)

Judging the Judge

There often seems to be confusion amongst students of *A Course in Miracles* on the subject of judgement. I have lost count of the number of times I have been asked about this in my workshops. I hear two basic questions: "I cannot see how we can stop judging. Don't we need to make judgements every day?" and "When does an observation become a judgement?"

Living in this world, we do indeed need to make judgements. The Song of Prayer says:

> *There are decisions to make here, and they must be made whether they be illusions or not.*
> (Song of Prayer, p. 2)

We need to determine, for example, where and when to cross the road by judging the distance and speed of approaching vehicles. Yet, when it comes to other people, there is a big difference between this kind of discernment and the negative value judgements of which the Course speaks.

There may be aspects and characteristics that we see in others, including persistent, negative traits that they do in fact possess. When we say someone is selfish, for example, it may be that they do tend to consider their interests above others. When we say that someone is unreliable, they may indeed consistently turn up late for important meetings or not do what they say they will do. In making these observations, however, we are not necessarily judging – unless we are!

The Course is talking about another kind of judgement, which only serves to reinforce the ego and which we are encouraged to let go of (forgive), in order to heal ourselves. This is the kind of negative judgement that hurts us first, because its intent is to evaluate the words and actions of others to convict them of being bad, evil, wrong, guilty, etc. When we judge another in any of these ways, we are judging ourselves. What we see and judge in another is what we do not want to acknowledge in ourselves. And, as we know, by holding the other person guilty in this way, we perpetuate guilt in ourselves (which is what the ego wants). This is the kind of judgement the Course is encouraging us to look at and let go of.

Thus, it is not wrong or unspiritual, for example, to prefer one school for your kids above another, or even to prefer one person to another (that is how we choose our friends), any more than preferring red wine to white, or tea to coffee. These are just preferences, and we cannot live in this world without them. Otherwise we would spend all day in the supermarket not being able to select our groceries, and we would never be able to decide where to go on holiday! But to make such choices is not to say white wine is evil or that coffee or Florida are wrong! Where we come unstuck is by judging ourselves – our friends, team, class, gender, country, or race – as superior, thereby condemning someone, perpetuating guilt and creating or reinforcing separation.

It is not unspiritual to have preferences in this world. We can have preferences without attachment and without rejecting. We can make choices between what is desirable and what is not without feeling guilty. It is not distrusting to check before stepping into the road that there is no oncoming traffic. We have to live in the world, while we remember we are not of this world.

A Course in Miracles does not say that we shouldn't judge; it says we cannot judge. Our hierarchy of preferences is, in fact, a hierarchy of illusions. While we do not have the capacity to make useful judgements, the Holy Spirit does. He can see the full picture, while we see only a fragment. By letting go of our judgements, we allow space for His.

As judgment shuts the mind against God's Teacher, so open-mind-

edness invites Him to come in.
(Manual, p. 16)

We can also invite Him to judge against the ego, the *"right use of judgment"*. (Text, p. 64) This is the kind of judgement, the Course says, which should be made, whereby He judges the ego, not as bad or evil, but as meaningless.

One Truth Looking Like Many

There were three schools of thought about Gary Renard's book *The Disappearance of the Universe*.

One group, whom we could call the disbelievers, doubted the truth of author Renard's story of teachings given to him by ascended masters, claiming that if it is not true, then it invalidates the whole book. The second group believed the story completely. The third group maintained that it was the message that mattered, not whether Renard's claims were true. (Renard, of course, has always maintained that he has told the truth.)

At one point in 2006, this debate became quite heated and spilled on to the Internet. Some quite defamatory articles were published, by both sides, in various ACIM journals in the US. The controversy was almost enough to make one want to find another spiritual path – one of peace and harmony!

A few years before that, the "Course world" was engulfed in a controversy that ended in a US court ruling that invalidated the Course's copyright. There were, again, at least two groups – those in favour of maintaining copyright and those who wanted it dissolved.

Nowadays, there are groups favouring particular Course teachers with different interpretations of the Course's message, most notably the Wapnick school; the Perry-Watson (Circle of Atonement) school; the Marianne Williamson school; the Endeavor Academy school; and the Gary Renard school.

There is only one Truth, but should we really be surprised that all these groups exist? No. Just look at the divisions in Christianity, which began within just a few decades of Jesus, over two thousand years ago. As we know, vicious and costly wars have been fought over these differences over the centuries.

And doctrinal differences don't arise only in Christianity. Virtually all religions and philosophies have experienced splits and the emergence of groups bitterly opposed to one another. There are different orders in Buddhism, Islam, and Judaism, even different Qigong (Ch'i Kung) schools – all, no doubt, thinking that they are doing things better than the others.

Should we be surprised? No. This is a very human tendency, but shouldn't students of *A Course in Miracles*, a teaching about Oneness and non-separation, be beyond all this? My feeling is that such splits are inevitable in a world that is founded on the thought of separation. A thought of separation can only result in separation, and that is true of anything or of any kind of community on the planet, sooner or later.

But surely, there must be another way? Yes, fortunately, there is. The central teaching of *A Course in Miracles*, the illusion that undoes all others, is forgiveness. We are called upon to forgive the differences, splits, disagreements, disputes and controversies. After all, it is either that or make them real and into a problem for which there is no solution.

Forgiving means that we see what is going on, without denial or "spiritualising" the situation, but we don't take it so seriously, as something to go to war over. We can begin to laugh at the ego's insanity, walk more lightly through the world, love our brothers – whatever their beliefs – and live the happy dream!

The Body Doesn't Mind

Consider these questions for a moment. Where is your mind? And where is your body? We tend to think that our body exists in the world and that our minds are located in some space inside our bodies, specifically in our brains. *A Course in Miracles*, however, says that everything, including the body, exists in the mind. The body is, in fact, merely a concept or idea in the mind. Bodies, therefore, do not do anything independently of mind, which is the only creative force.

The Course says: *"Sickness is a defense against the truth."* (Workbook, p. 257) All illness stems from our body identification. One could say that we are attempting to do with the body what cannot be done, i.e. using it as our identity, who we are. This erroneous belief is an attack on the truth that we remain as we were created by God: pure spirit and pure love, like Him. This attack is the symptom of a sick mind, and sick minds produce sick bodies.

Sickness is not an accident. Like all defenses, it is an insane device for self-deception. And like all the rest, its purpose is to hide reality, attack it... or reduce it to a little pile of unassembled parts.
(Workbook, p. 257)

Sickness is a decision. It is not a thing that happens to you, quite unsought, which makes you weak and brings you suffering. It is a choice you make, a plan you lay, when for an instant truth arises in your own deluded mind... Now are you sick, that truth may go away and threaten your establishments no more.
(Workbook, p. 258)

Sickness tells us that we are a body. The ego (the belief in separation) uses the sickness that it has deliberately but unconsciously made to keep away the truth that threatens it. The preoccupation with symptoms and our attempts to be healed keep our attention fixed on the body and away from our minds – where we could make a different decision.

How do you think that sickness can succeed in shielding you from truth? Because it proves the body is not separate from you, and so you must be separate from the truth. You suffer pain because the body does, and in this pain are you made one with it... and the strange, haunting thought that you might be something beyond this little pile of dust silenced and stilled.
(Workbook, p. 258)

Sickness is isolation. For it seems to keep one self apart from all the rest, to suffer what the others do not feel. It gives the body final power to make the separation real, and keep the mind in solitary prison, split apart... by a solid wall of sickened flesh...
(Workbook, p. 261)

We think that we are the victims of what the body does to us. We may even believe that we deserve to be sick because we are bad and deserve punishment. But we've entirely forgotten that we have done all this to ourselves. Forgetting renders our decisions beyond correction.

It is this quick forgetting of the part you play in making your 're-ality' that makes defenses seem to be beyond your own control... Your not remembering is but the sign that this decision still remains in force... Defenses must make facts unrecognisable.
(Workbook, p. 257)

I acknowledge the presence of this thought in myself. On rare occasions, dimly and distantly, I have caught the thought of actually *wanting* to be sick. It is an attack thought; it asserts that

I am a victim of the world. The thought of sickness claims to show how tough it has been for me, and that I am right to believe that no one understands. All this is quite insane.

If we believe that sickness is done to us by our bodies and that, in turn, external agents (viruses, germs, etc) have done it to our bodies, we will also believe that healing is done for us by external agents (pills, potions, herbs, crystals, doctors, healers, etc). In truth, if mind is the only creative force it, too, is the healing agent. Our minds simply invest certain external agents with the power to heal. Like everything else in the physical world, they have no power in themselves. If we want to get well, we will do so. If we want to remain sick, it will be so. If we believe a remedial agent will work, it will. Otherwise, it will fail.

Accepting ourselves as God created us – fully, completely and absolutely – will be the end of sickness because it will be the end of body identification. Our decisions for sickness are not true and they have no meaning. Yet we have believed them. When we accept this entirely, healing will be immediate. Until then, we can use each situation involving sickness to remind ourselves of what we have chosen to believe, and do to ourselves, so that we can eventually make a better choice. Love, truth and healing are available to us right now and merely wait for our acceptance.

No one can heal unless he understands what purpose sickness seems to serve. For then he understands as well its purpose has no meaning. Being causeless and without a meaningful intent of any kind, it cannot be at all. When this is seen, healing is automatic. It dispels this meaningless illusion by the same approach that carries all of them to truth, and merely leaves them there to disappear. (Workbook, p. 257)

Let us bring healing closer by telling ourselves:

Sickness is a defense against the truth. I will accept the truth of what I am, and let my mind be wholly healed today.
(Workbook, p. 259)

It's Not Fair!

Walking past a community playground recently, I noticed some kids on a climbing frame. Then I heard one say (you can likely hear the whiny, child-like voice): *"It's not fair. I'm not playing any more!"*

I realised that adults say things like that too. We use grown-up language, but we've internalised the same kind of thinking: *"It's not fair, I don't like it."* And we stamp our foot and sulk. People go off in a huff, resign, refuse to cooperate or play, because they don't like something that has happened.

Hearing those children reminded me of what some people in an organisation I am involved with had done a week or so before. They left the group angrily because they did not like the way change was handled. I have acted similarly, for all sorts of reasons, many times.

A Course in Miracles says: *"I am never upset for the reason I think"* (Workbook, p. 8) and *"I see only the past."* (Workbook, p. 11) Everything I am not happy about in this moment is my internal four-year-old kicking and screaming in the past about what he lost and was not able to recapture. I may think it is about what so-and-so did just now, but really it is about something that happened long ago.

Workbook Lesson 7 in the Course (*"I see only the past"*) goes on to say that this

> is the reason why nothing that you see means anything... why you have given everything you see all the meaning that it has for you... why you do not understand anything you see... why your thoughts do not mean anything... why you are never upset for the reason you think

and

why you are upset because you see something that is not there.
(Workbook, p. 11)

The reason we get upset is not what we think. Ultimately, traced far enough back, it is because of the false belief that we have separated from God – which we feel guilty for, but project on to the world that seemingly did it to us. Thus, we are not responsible; he, she or it that caused it is the guilty one. Events that happen to us, such as childhood traumas, reinforce this mistaken idea that we are victims, unfairly treated by an unkind world ("It's not fair").

This is why *A Course in Miracles* also says: *"Beware of the temptation to perceive yourself unfairly treated."* (Text, p. 563)

Everything we believe is rooted in time. Something that occurs now reminds us of a similar event in the past, thus confirming our beliefs. Then we drag the past into the present, recreating the past over and over again – until, through forgiveness, we can rewrite the past and create a new present, unencumbered by past erroneous thinking.

Lesson 7 gives a simple example of looking at a cup. We do not see the cup as it is, only recalling past experiences of cups, picking them up, drinking from them and what that feels like and so on. The lesson asks:

What do you know about this cup except what you learned in the past? You would have no idea what this cup is, except for your past learning. Do you, then, really see it?
(Workbook, p. 11)

Similarly, when circumstances occur, or people behave in a certain way, are you seeing them as they truly are, or is your past learning colouring your perception and the way you react?

The internal person, kicking and screaming in the past, is our neurosis. However, with awareness and forgiveness, we can learn to choose something different when we automatically react to people and situations.

Next time you catch yourself reacting, ask yourself what your reaction is really about, why you are really upset, then forgive and let it go. Finally, you might like to say to yourself: *"I feel safe and I like you. Let's play!"* (in a happy, child-like voice). Rewrite that well-worn, tired old playground script.

Relationship Rollercoaster

There is undoubtedly something wonderful about being in a relationship that truly makes you happy, fills you up, makes you feel alive and vibrant. I think it is what we all want.

I have had relationships like this. And when I do, I want them to go on forever – though beneath the thrill is the lingering fear that they will not last, and how terrible I am going to feel when they come to an end. I know the devastation, loss, emptiness and loneliness that follow – the low that follows the high.

So, what causes us to live like this? What creates this roller-coaster ride? Is the answer just to keep moving on, always finding someone new to fulfil your needs? If so, we are searching for love that we believe we do not have and that must be found in someone else.

Everyone who believes that the ego is salvation seems to be intensely engaged in the search for love. Yet the ego, though encouraging [this] very actively, makes one proviso; do not find it.
(Text, p. 223)

Over and over and over this ritual is enacted. And it is never completed, nor ever will be completed.
(Text, p. 343)

I have come to realise that everything a relationship appeared to be bringing me – love, connection, wholeness – I have already, in an abundant and inexhaustible supply. What I attempt to get from it, I already am! Rather than looking outside myself, I can turn within and find it there. And it cannot be taken away from me, or be withheld in any way. So there is good reason to buy *myself* a bunch of roses, or a box of Black Magic and crack open a bottle of champagne!

I am not talking about a mere intellectual understanding of what *A Course in Miracles* tells us is our true nature. I mean that we can actually feel it and know it in the core of our being and tangibly in our bodies here in the world. When we feel whole in our gut and full up, we have got it (and it is not just the Black Magic!). We *are* what we seek. *"God is but Love, and therefore so am I."* (Workbook, pp. 329–35)

It is from this place that a holy relationship can form. *"A holy relationship starts from a different premise. Each one has looked within and seen no lack."* (Text, p. 467) In truth, the only kind of love that is real and genuine is that which flows from this endless place of no lack within us.

There is no other love that can satisfy you, because there is no other love. This is the only love that is fully given and fully returned. Being complete, it asks nothing. Being wholly pure, everyone joined in it has everything. This is not the basis for any relationship in which the ego enters. For every relationship on which the ego embarks is special.
(Text, p. 317)

We bring to the relationship a quiet, inner celebration of our holiness and a wish only to give to the partnership. Since what you give is increased, our sense of love and abundance is increased and, with it, the lingering fear of loss is gone.

How lovely and how holy is your relationship, with the truth shining upon it!... The universe within you stands with you, together with your brother. And Heaven looks with love on what is joined in it, along with its Creator.
(Text, pp. 374–5)

Letting the Guilt(y) Go

How did you react to the news that Jon Venables (convicted, at the age of eleven, of the abduction, torture and murder of toddler James Bulger in 1993) had been recalled to prison for breaking the terms of his parole? I was shocked at the venom still directed at this man by the media and public, seventeen years on from the appalling events. The sense of outrage was understandable at the time. But the lingering grievance – the idea that this man should forever be made to suffer and pay for what he did as a child – shook me.

But, then, it is guilt not love that makes the world go round. The ego's desire to project blame, even to the extent of having 'public hate figures', is seemingly never-ending.

I often quote the case of Myra Hindley, one of the Moors Murderers, who served a life sentence for the murder, with Ian Brady, of five children in the 1960s. Whenever there was talk of releasing her from prison, the public debate evoked similar reaction to the Venables case. Usually, the mother of one of the victims was interviewed and asked what she thought. The response would normally be something along the lines of: "I think that woman should rot in hell for what she did." Again, from a human perspective, that feeling is understandable, but – terrible as her loss was – the fact that she had carried that anger for forty years was just as tragic.

These are extreme cases I'm using to illustrate the point that holding on to grievances is what egos like to do. We are attached to our stories of what happened, what it means (about others and ourselves), our sense of being wronged and our justified, self-righteous anger.

As the Course suggests, we project on to others the content of our minds. I submit that if we are honest, we will find, in our own minds, thoughts of abuse, victimisation and murder.

Although most of us do not act on these thoughts, how often have we had thoughts of wanting to hurt others? When someone exclaims: "I want to kill him!" is that not betraying a murderous thought? *A Course in Miracles* contains pages of graphic descriptions of the ego's murderous intentions.

The guilt and shame we feel about these thoughts is then projected on to those who do act them out. We are being called upon to forgive and thus heal our own minds, rather than condemn and keep the whole scheme going.

I once attended a talk given by Jo Berry and Patrick Magee. Jo is the daughter of a Conservative MP, Sir Anthony Berry, who was killed by the Brighton bomb in 1984; Pat was the IRA member who planted the bomb. Theirs is an amazing story of reconciliation and forgiveness. They talked about their similarities and differences that still remain between them, about how they have learned to understand and appreciate one another and become friends.

Living in London in the late 1970s and 1980s, when the IRA set off bombs in the city including those at Harrods, Hyde Park and Victoria Station, I had felt under attack. It was difficult being in the presence of Pat Magee. I had some forgiving to do. When he appeared, at one point during their presentation, to justify the use of violence for political ends, I wanted to walk out.

But I stayed and was able to see him differently. I saw his struggle and inner conflict, as he came to terms with his past and where he is today, sitting next to the daughter of one of his victims. I felt compassion for his sense of guilt and really heard him when he asked the audience what we would have done living in similar circumstances.

At the end of the evening, I was able to shake Pat's hand, not because I agreed with him but because I felt it would help me find my own inner peace, to forgive and to let go of the past. It was quite an evening!

I have found peace and wish the same for all who struggle to let go of traumatic stories, grievances and righteous indignation at past wrongs, and who do the inner work necessary to see the inherent innocence of everyone.

The Expansion of Love

Living in this world, do we really know what *love* is? We certainly think we do. But is it all roses, chocolates and Valentine cards? Or is love simply caring for people and being kind? In some quarters, love is synonymous with sex ('making love'). Can we really grasp the full magnitude of Love? Or do we merely experience the tiniest hints of the Love that is All?

In Lency Spezzano's book *Make Way For Love*, she talks about opening our hearts to experiencing more love. I think this is a process over time, as ACIM would put it, of undoing the blocks to the awareness of love's presence. I have found that *A Course in Miracles* has made a greater contribution to this process than anything else in my life. As I have opened my heart to allow a greater experience of love, so the love I have felt has expanded my heart and allowed me to open more. I think the Course is concerned less with what we might call 'little' love (the kind of love we experience in our relationships from day to day), but more with 'big' Love (the Love of God, our ultimate Reality).

I spent much of my life feeling lonely and unloved. It was not that I *was* unloved, but rather that I did not feel it. I had loving parents, and friends who seemed to like me, but I felt disconnected and isolated from them. I had withdrawn from life, because of guilt and pain. I felt that there was no love there for me, but that's because I was blocking it and not receiving what was available. I did not know how to open and receive. My ego had an investment in keeping me small and separate, of course. And even though I thought there was no love out there for me, I kept looking.

In the world of scarcity, love has no meaning and peace is impossible. For gain and loss are both accepted, and so no one is aware that perfect love is in him.

(Text, p. 315)

I sought consolation, as many of us do, in shallow and fleeting relationships, and by finding substitutes for love by busying myself in the world. I concluded that love was for others, but not for me. I tried to resign myself to the idea that I must have a different role to play in life.

... you are unwilling to accept that perfect love is in you. And so you seek without for what you cannot find without.
(Text, p. 314)

... in the holy instant, free of the past, you see that love is in you, and you have no need to look without and snatch love guiltily from where you thought it was.
(Text, p. 314)

Eventually, I started my journey of metaphysical discovery, and began to slowly embrace more of life. Some years later, I had the recognition that *A Course in Miracles* was my path, and I knew that somehow I would find my way back. Sure enough, many incredible shifts have taken place, but one stands out especially in my mind. It occurred when I reached Workbook Lesson 127: *"There is no love but God's."* (Workbook, p. 230) I suddenly realised that, for years, I had only been looking for love in one particular form, that of an intimate, committed, romantic relationship. What I now recognised was that there is only *one* Love.

Perhaps you think that different kinds of love are possible. Perhaps you think there is a kind of love for this, a kind for that; a way of loving one, another way of loving still another. Love is one. It has no separate parts and no degrees; no kinds nor levels, no divergencies and no distinctions. It is like itself, unchanged throughout.

It never alters with a person or a circumstance. It is the Heart of
God, and also of His Son.
(Workbook, p. 230)

Whether it is love of family members, friends, colleagues,
acquaintances, partners, or God, it is all the same thing. Love is
constant, in whatever form it comes. It comes in different
packages, but the gift is identical. I was looking for it in only one
kind of package, but it was there all the time, in many different
shaped and sized packages, all around me. What I had been
looking for, and thinking was not for me, had been there all
along, simply unrecognised. It was there in *all* my relationships:
friends, family, colleagues, etc. I realised that I did not have to
search any more. All I needed to do was to relax and enjoy what
was already mine – in abundance!

You cannot enter into real relationships with any of God's Sons un-
less you love them all equally. Love is not special. If you single out
part of the Sonship for your love, you are imposing guilt on all your
relationships and making them unreal. You can love only as God
loves. Seek not to love unlike Him, for there is no love apart from
His. Until you recognise that this is true, you will have no idea what
love is like.
(Text, p. 265)

From that point on, I did relax. I stopped searching and felt in
touch with how much love there was in my life. I was not looking
for that 'special someone' to make me complete (but neither was
I resisting). I felt like a whole, complete person, whether I was on
my own or not. It made no difference to me whether I was in a
relationship or not. Love filled me and nurtured me. I was
content.

Now I am on my way. I feel that my heart is growing every
day. My capacity for love is expanding. I am also less defensive,

more at peace, more centred, relaxed and intimate with people, and much happier. I am ready for a new kind of relationship now. And that is all it takes – a waking up to what has always been mine, and for me to say "Yes" to life.

Maybe this is just that tiniest glimpse of Love mentioned at the beginning of this section, but behind it there is infinitely more. I know it is there and it is mine, because it is *who* I am and Who my Creator is.

Love waits on welcome, not on time, and the real world is but your welcome of what always was. Therefore the call of joy is in it, and your glad response is your awakening to what you have not lost.
(Text, pp. 255–6)

Take heart.

… there can never be a difference in what you really are and what love is. Love's meaning is your own, and shared by God Himself. For what you are is what He is. There is no love but His, and what He is, is everything there is. There is no limit placed upon Himself, and so are you unlimited as well.
(Workbook, p. 230)

Counselling and Forgiveness

Although I have no training or experience in formal counselling, increasingly, over the years people have come to me for advice and help with their personal problems. I have never thought of myself as being a good listener, yet I seem to be able to offer something helpful.

What has become apparent to me from all these calls for help is that the way forward is always forgiveness in some form. In my book (*A Course in Miracles*), everything boils down to forgiveness in the end – forgiveness of self, others, one's life circumstances, or God – regardless of the particular stories told by different individuals. Perhaps people should avoid coming to me, because I always offer them the last thing their egos want to hear – forgiveness! They would usually rather blame: "Oh damn," they say, "I knew you were going to say forgiveness."

> *… there can be no form of suffering that fails to hide an unforgiving thought. Nor can there be a form of pain forgiveness cannot heal.*
> (Workbook, p. 380)

Here are two examples:

David was plagued by lethargy and lack of motivation. His life was directionless. Every time he entered a new job or yet another new relationship, he found some way of sabotaging it. He had tried this romance, then that; this career move, then that. Yet each time, he managed to undermine his success in some way. "That wasn't right," he would say and move on to the next 'answer'. Eventually, he reached the point of believing that nothing would work and that he was, somehow, fundamentally flawed.

When I asked David what the pay-off was in these repeated failures, we eventually whittled it down to proving his belief that his parents failed in his upbringing. He believed they never offered him enough support or guidance. And he was certifying their guilt to himself, over and over again, with his string of disasters. He believed he was a failure and that his parents were to blame. Forgiveness of both could have shifted this stuckness for good.

Andrew felt anger, sadness, confusion, guilt and loneliness in what he saw as a loveless marriage. He was jealous of his wife's attraction to another man whom she met in an evening class, and felt abandoned and rejected. He and his wife had agreed to separate, but continued to live under the same roof for the sake of the children. The kids picked up on the gulf between their parents nonetheless, and were acting out by bed-wetting, misbehaving and even becoming violent. Andrew took on more and more work in an attempt to cover up his sense of worthlessness. He was desperate to find a way out of the craziness he found himself in, blaming both himself and his wife for the situation. He realised that forgiveness could transform the whole mess.

> The unforgiving mind is full of fear, and offers love no room to be itself... is sad, without the hope of respite and release from pain... The unforgiving mind is torn with doubt, confused about itself and all it sees; afraid and angry, weak and blustering, afraid to go ahead, afraid to stay, afraid to waken or go to sleep... The unforgiving mind sees no mistakes, but only sins... The unforgiving mind is in despair, without the prospect of a future which can offer anything but more despair.
> (Workbook, p. 214)

Forgiveness offered a simple solution for both David and Andrew. Forgiveness is the core tool in the Course's training programme. Why? Because it works – if you practise it and *truly* wish it to work. But it will fail if you actually want something else instead.

Forgiveness does not magically change one's external circumstances. It is an undoing, a letting-go of our belief that mistakes are "sins". That means the letting-go of our erroneous beliefs, not merely about what has been done to us, but about who and what we are. Forgiveness brings the realisation that these beliefs are not true and never were; they were simply mistakes. Forgiveness is not fixing, repairing or making our beliefs better so that they can be proven true. Instead, it is letting go of fear, defensiveness and grievances. Forgiveness restores peace to your mind and the knowledge of who you are in truth, innocence, perfection, divinity and love.

> *What could you want forgiveness cannot give? Do you want peace... happiness, a quiet mind, a certainty of purpose... a sense of worth and beauty that transcends the world... care and safety... the warmth of sure protection always... quietness that cannot be disturbed, a gentleness that never can be hurt... All this forgiveness offers you, and more.*
> (Workbook, p. 217)

Every process, prayer, meditation and exercise must result in forgiveness if it is to be effective in healing. *"Miracles are natural signs of forgiveness. Through miracles you accept God's forgiveness by extending it to others."* (Text, p. 4) So don't come asking my advice if you are looking for some other solution!

Variety or Peace?

Variety, says the old maxim, is the spice of life. And on a certain limited, worldly level it is probably true. However, it is also true that "spice" does not result in inner peace or happiness.

I have long lived by the idea of the spice of life, filling my time with lots of exciting and varied things. I used to say that I would try anything once, but it went beyond that. It was almost as if I had to try *everything* – especially anything new or different. New places, new parts of the world, new relationships, anything that might result in 'thrills and spills', maybe even 'cheap thrills'. I was constantly shifting my attention from one thing to another, collecting experiences. I wanted to try them all – for the 'buzz'.

I am sure this plays out, in some way, for all of us. The ego encourages us to fill our lives with exciting stuff and tells us that it will be fulfilling. The ego is always on the search.

The illusion persists that, although [the hope of salvation] *has always failed, there is still grounds for hope in other places and in other things. Another person will yet serve better; another situation will yet offer success.*
(Workbook, p. 121)

However, what the ego offers is not the true fulfilment it appears to be. It is just adrenalin. It does not work for more than, perhaps, a few moments – as long as the 'thrill of the seduction' or a honeymoon. A temporary rush appeals to the ego's drive to *"Seek but do not find"* (Manual, p. 34), whereby it is always looking for the thing to fill the void but never finding it, and always keeping us away from the void.

I have realised that, in seeking the spice, I have been missing or even avoiding the 'sugar', the sweetness that lies in every moment, if I would only stop long enough to recognise and appreciate it.

The result [of the ego's thinking] *is a weaving, changing pattern that never rests and is never still. It shifts unceasingly across the mirror of your mind, and the reflections of Heaven last but a moment and grow dim, as darkness blots them out.*
(Text, pp. 293–4)

Interestingly, it was once suggested to me by Chuck Spezzano that the diabetic condition I have is a metaphor (as all disease is) for my inability to "take in the sweetness of life." Chuck was referring to my inability to fully accept the love that I truly am – and that we all are. (I am not unique in this. It's everyone's struggle.)

Many philosophies highlight the practice of being in the present moment, stopping the chase, fully experiencing and appreciating the eternal 'now'. This practice, combined with forgiveness and a total acceptance of what is, is a precursor for experiencing what *A Course in Miracles* calls the holy instant.

Being in the now and taking in the sweetness of life is dependent on nothing. There is nothing more we have to do, find, possess, or achieve. We can be there right now, with whatever is going on for us. Stopping and *being*, without judgement, is all that's required. This is where your Self is, where Love is found and where God is:

The part of your mind in which truth abides is in constant communication with God... It is the other part of your mind that functions in the world and... is constantly distracted, disorganized and highly uncertain... The part that is listening to the Voice for God is calm, always at rest and wholly certain.
(Workbook, p. 78)

The ego will still be there, doing what it believes to be its job of pulling us away from the sweetness. "Try this," it will say. "That looks exciting." At times I will succumb to its temptation. Yet I know, now, that I would rather have the sugar than the spice any day.

> *Let* [temptations] *go... till they disappear from sight, far, far outside of you. And turn you to the stately calm within, where in holy stillness dwells the living God.*
> (Text, pp. 373–4)

Letting Go of Nothing

One of the hardest things for me to do is 'let go'. That's because in the world, being identified with the ego, I have invested everything with a reality and an importance that it does not, in fact, possess.

A Course in Miracles says that the world is an illusion, a dream or hallucination that we are all having, and is without any reality whatsoever. It is no more, and no less, than an "out-picturing" of our internal thoughts and beliefs.

Every attachment we have keeps us hooked into this illusion, in a prison of our own making. It is not just our attachment to people, possessions and relationships, but also holding on to our plans, positions and status, everyday roles in the world, our ideas about how things should look and our wanting to be right. I am talking about anything we desire, need, or believe that without which we will be inadequate.

There is nothing wrong with any of these ideas, roles, or relationships, or simply 'playing' with them for a while; it is the *attachment* to any of them that does not work. The danger surfaces when we do not get what we want, or if we have it and then lose it. Then comes the pain, in direct measure to the degree of attachment. The moment we *must* have something in order to be happy, we are no longer free. As it says in the Bible, if we have built our house on sand, then when the sand gets washed away (as it inevitably will in an unreliable world of constant change), the foundations will collapse. We need to build our house on rock, rather than all the sands of the illusory world.

Disillusionment follows when we achieve, obtain or gain something and it doesn't make the difference we thought it would. That's because we were attached to an illusion in the first place. We turn to what the Course calls *idols* when we are really looking for God's Love. Maybe we have to attempt to follow a few false leads before we finally realise that there must be a better way.

Our illusions appear to hold out so much promise of fulfilment and joy, yet deliver so much pain. The Course says that as long as we continue to look to the world for our salvation, and value what we see out there, we will be disappointed. To attain the Kingdom of Heaven we must be free of our burdens. In the Bible, Jesus said, "my yoke is easy and my burden is light" because he had nothing to weigh him down.

In truth, we are lacking nothing. In God, we have everything of value that we could ever want. *"Illusion can but seem to hold in chains the holy Son of God."* (Workbook, p. 292) *"Dreams are not a worthy guide for you who are God's Son."* (Workbook, p. 293)

I find it hard to let go in peace. I find it much easier to make someone into an enemy, or to view a situation as undesirable so that I can separate and say, "Thank God that's over and I'm out of there."

But this is not the same as letting go. I think in this way when I am still hooked into, and 'at the effect' of, the person or the situation. The trick is to keep your peace and to realise that you have no claim over the person or control over the situation. Instead you are being given a gift, an opportunity, as always, to release your burden.

In practice, however, we often feel as if we're being asked to give up something of value when faced with letting go. It *seems* as if a sacrifice is being called for. However, it cannot be a sacrifice to let illusions go. In the "Development of Trust" section of the Manual for Teachers, the Course says that a

period of undoing… need not be painful, but it usually is so experienced. It seems as if things are being taken away, and it is rarely understood initially that their lack of value is merely being recognized.
(Manual, p. 10)

Yet, the mere fact that we are being called on to let go tells us that we are, currently, holding on to something or someone. In that moment, we do not want to, and the mind is split. We may know intellectually that we have to let go, yet emotionally we want to hang on for dear life. We may be clinging on by our fingernails to keep our dream alive, or engaged in yet one more vain attempt to grab hold of our illusion. I think we have to be honest about how much we want to hold on before we can make a better choice and let go.

It is our ego believing in the illusion that wants to hold on. We cannot, of ourselves, simply let go. So we need help from outside the ego thought system. Fortunately, that help is at hand. The Holy Spirit will answer our prayers and requests for help. And only a *"little willingness"* (Text, pp. 380–1) is required:

"Let me forgive [this person] and release them to You."

"Help me to let go of my attachment to [this situation] being what I wanted."

"Help me to step back and let You lead the way."

I am reminded of the story about a man climbing alone in the mountains. He came to the edge of a precipice, looked over the side, got dizzy, lost his balance and fell. Quickly he reached out and grabbed the branch of a small tree. Suspended hundreds of feet in the air and unable to think of anything better to do, he cried out for help. "Is anybody there?"

There was a long silence. Then, a voice from the blue said: "It's all right, my son. I'm here. I will take care of you. Just let go."

There was another long silence and the man replied: "Is anybody else there?"

The World Is Witness

One of the most important teachings from *A Course in Miracles* is that

The world... is the witness to your state of mind, the outside picture of an inward condition. As a man thinketh, so does he perceive. Therefore, seek not to change the world, but choose to change your mind about the world. Perception is a result and not a cause.
(Text, p. 445)

What this means is that "the world" is only our experience of it, and that our experience is dependent on our thoughts. This is not the way the world thinks, but it is the way that Course students are taught to think.

It is so tempting to believe that we will be happy when we get a new job, a new house, a new relationship (or any relationship), or when we get some money, when so-and-so stops bothering us, when we get a new government or move to a different country, and so on. But what we find when we attempt to change something in the world 'out there', in the world of form, is that after the initial novelty has worn off we are back where we started, with the empty feeling that something is still missing in our lives.

The problem is that, regardless of what aspect of our lives we may have changed, we are still the same person. We think it is the job, the relationship, the car, or whatever, that we are looking for, but what we are really looking for is love, happiness, fulfilment and, above all, peace of mind. Those experiences don't come from outside ourselves. Changing forms and circumstances are like rearranging the deckchairs on the Titanic, as the old saying goes.

It is not that we cannot enjoy the things of this world. Of

course we can and we do. It is not that the things of the world are either bad or good. It's just that they are nothing; they comprise a blank canvas on to which we project all the meaning they have for us.

All the problems of life arise from focusing our attention on what is happening outside; on what we are *doing*, and on things or circumstances. If we are not happy, the answer is not about changing any of that – moving the furniture; it *is* about "working miracles" on the inside. Choosing to change your mind about the world is what's required.

Once the inner transformation is underway, incredible changes will occur, even in external circumstances over which it seems you have no control.

I have experienced seeing things change when I change my thoughts about them. For a few years I have quietly nursed the idea of living in Australia or California, simply for the hot weather. On a visit to the United States in 1994, however, I realised how much I like living in London and how much I love England and the English countryside, even if the sun is not always shining. Therefore, I dropped all my ideas of leaving and consciously chose that where I live is where I want to be.

From the moment of making that decision, my level of appreciation dramatically increased. London literally seemed to have changed for the better before my very eyes. I enjoyed my friends and my lifestyle here much more than before. Incredibly, even the city itself seemed to be cleaner and brighter. I noticed beautiful, interesting and quaint old buildings, which I had somehow not seen before. In summer, there seemed to be flowers everywhere (I think Westminster City Council spent a fortune putting up hanging baskets); there was suddenly so much colour. Continental-style pavement cafes seemed to have sprung up everywhere and the pubs seemed to have a better range of beers (something I love!). Even our summer weather was wonderful that year, while the autumn was the mildest for years.

I chose to be happy and, sure enough, I was happy. It is so simple. The challenge now is to apply the same principle to the rest of my life.

Praying, therefore, means asking for peace of mind, for our minds to be healed, rather than asking for specific things to be manifested. Better still, it becomes an expression of gratitude for what is, and nothing more. One of my own prayers is: "Dear God, please heal my mind that I may come to know You, that Your Will be done, that I may be happy, that I may be at peace. Thank you. Amen."

Just relax and let the Holy Spirit take care of the inner realms. The Course says that we do not even know what is in our best interests, but He does. He knows that what we *really* want is peace and happiness, and that is what He brings. Try it. It works!

For what you see is merely how you elect to meet your goal. [Hallucinations] *are the means by which the outside world, projected from within, adjusts to sin and seems to witness to its reality. It still is true that nothing is without. Yet upon nothing are all projections made. When you have looked on what seemed terrifying, and seen it change to sights of loveliness and peace; when you have looked on scenes of violence and death, and watched them change to quiet views of gardens under open skies, with clear, life-giving water running happily beside them in dancing brooks that never waste away; who need persuade you to accept the gift of vision?*
(Text, pp. 443–4)

Everyday Holy Instants

In 2004, I was invited to go to Los Angeles to speak at an *A Course in Miracles* conference on the same platform as Jerry Jampolsky and Beverly Hutchinson McNeff. Flattery and excitement at the prospect of a free flight to southern California kept me going for several months. They wanted me to tell them all about what is happening with the Course in the UK. Easy! Then I looked again at the subject of the conference – the holy instant – and panicked. What did I know about holy instants?

I could remember two major holy instants – one which set me on the spiritual path in the first place, and another which resulted in the beginning of the Miracle Network ten years ago. But ongoing, everyday holy instants? I could recall many fleeting moments of forgiveness, connection or joining with people (particularly during workshops), elevated moments during prayer or meditation, moments of inspiration and heightened awareness in nature. But, in my panic, I could not think of a single incident of revelation or altered state of awareness that would make an interesting story!

Holy instants are potential in every second. *"The holy instant is this instant and every instant. The one you want it to be it is... You must decide when it is."* (Text, p. 309)

They are temporary, transcendental or profound spiritual experiences, which are either momentary or, occasionally, extended. They are about being 'in the now', in the timeless, changeless present.

Fear is not of the present, but only of the past and future, which do not exist... And the present extends forever. It is so beautiful and so clean and free of guilt that nothing but happiness is there. No darkness is remembered, and immortality and joy are now.
(Text, pp. 302–3)

The holy instant is a moment in which we briefly leave the past and our normal thought processes and experience something 'outside the box' of normal consciousness. Sometimes, the experience of truly joining another person in their vulnerability and honesty brings the recognition of truth that transcends both.

The holy instant is the Holy Spirit's most useful learning device for teaching you love's meaning. For its purpose is to suspend judgment entirely... Judgment becomes impossible without the past.
(Text, p. 312)

The experience can be one of bliss, love, light, peace and oneness.

Can you imagine what it means to have no cares, no worries, no anxieties, but merely to be perfectly calm and quiet all the time?
(Text, p. 301)

If it was my ego telling me to dismiss the experiences I have had, this same voice of fear and doubt was preventing more holy instants that were available to me. Could I, somehow, open up more in order to initiate them? It occurred to me that, to paraphrase the Introduction to the ACIM Text, the holy instant is beyond what can be taught and our aim is to remove the blocks to the awareness of its existence.

If this is so, what were my blocks? My list included my ego's preoccupation with planning for the future, its love affair with guilt from the past, its constant replaying of the *if only's* and the *what could have been's,* and the holding of grievances, resentments and anger towards others.

All these blocks stand in the way of the holy instant. My job is to undo them, after which I will automatically gain an awareness allowing me to be wholly present. What is required then is the acceptance of what is already there and mine. Asking the Holy Spirit for help turns my attention away from the problem, toward a more open and receptive state.

My work of undoing the blocks is ongoing. My part is in this preparation, in being ready and willing to accept my inheritance. The Holy Spirit will then play His part, as the active agent in bringing about my experience of another state of mind.

It takes far longer to teach you to be willing to give Him this than for Him to use this tiny instant to offer you the whole of Heaven.
(Text, p. 303)

In the holy instant, I see beyond the body's limitations to the place of unlimited and total communication. Seeing beyond the body means seeing beyond guilt, separation and attack as means of getting my needs met. The body is given another purpose to the one for which it was made by the ego.

Holy instants are where miracles happen.

For the instant of holiness is shared, and cannot be yours alone. Remember, then, when you are tempted to attack a brother, that his instant of release is yours. Miracles are the instants of release you offer, and will receive.
(Text, p. 303)

They are my release from littleness and the realisation of my true magnitude, where I remember that: *"I am as God created me."* (Workbook pp. 164–5, 199–200, 307)

In my holy instants, my answers are already there, waiting. All things are answered and there is no conflict.

In quietness are all things answered, and is every problem quietly resolved... God must have given you a way of reaching to another state of mind in which the answer is already there. Such is the holy instant.

(Text, pp. 574–5)

Inspiration and true creativity are born here, too. There is the recognition of what is true and real, by which I am changed and made capable of carrying truth back into the world to offer gifts to others.

It is here that miracles are laid; to be returned by you from holy instants you receive... to all who see the light that lingers in your face. What is the face of Christ but his who went a moment into timelessness, and brought a clear reflection of the unity he felt an instant back to bless the world?
(Workbook, pp. 324–5)

Choosing Fear or Love

Consider this for a moment: Do you think that this is a world based on love and joy, or one based on fear?

A Course in Miracles tells us that this is an ego-generated world: that is, a world which was made out of separation and the fear that resulted from it. Let us look at the evidence for this in our everyday lives and activities.

Every day we wake up, feed ourselves out of fear that we might go hungry, clothe ourselves against the fear of getting cold (or being arrested for indecent exposure!) and go to work to earn a living to stave off the fear of not having enough money to survive. We take out insurance policies (fear of theft, fire, illness, death, etc); put our seatbelts on in the car (fear of injury or of being caught not wearing them); watch the speed limit (fear); watch the car in front (fear), and so on. We are careful to eat a balanced and healthy diet, take regular exercise and we will go to the doctor when we feel unwell (all in response to various fears of our body disintegrating). We educate our children and strive to get ahead at work, for fear of being poor or outclassed. We may seek relationships out of fear of being alone and may even marry for this reason. We may call our friends regularly to reassure ourselves that we are still loved. We buy books, televisions and videos to keep the fear of boredom at bay.

When you really consider it objectively, it is hard to find anything we do in this world that is not fear-based. In nature, too, all life competes to survive. The apparent law of the jungle is that you have to compete and defend, or die. The fight-or-flight reflex along with finding shelter, reproducing, and feeding are all survival-driven (fear) instincts. Just consider all the defence and attack mechanisms that nature has evolved: camouflage, biting, stinging, poisoning, etc. Fear, fear, fear.

On a trip to Africa, I watched some geckos on my ceiling. They would move six inches, then stop and remain motionless for some minutes before darting forward another six inches. They were always checking that they were safe and that there were no predators around. When walking in the bush, I always ensured that I wore my boots, in case there were snakes; I took steps against mosquitoes at night; I killed a large spider I found in my bathroom with a broom handle in case it was poisonous. Fear, fear, fear. *"When you are afraid of anything, you are acknowledging its power to hurt you."* (Text, p. 19)

On my trip, I also observed my friend's three children. It was fascinating to watch their powerful egos at work. If one of the children received something that the others did not, all hell broke loose. If one child started playing with a toy, suddenly the other two would want to play with it too, because of their fear of missing out. Fear, fear, fear.

Now, there is nothing wrong with any of this. Fear is not bad; it's just the way we have set up the world. As long as we believe that we can be robbed, get ill, be attacked, or fall prey to an accident, we might prefer to take precautions and keep our insurance policies. Doing otherwise may only *increase* our fears.

Since the entire world is a result of the original error of believing that we could be separate from God, the guilt and fear following on from that error will always be with us. There is no cure for fear in the world. *The Sunday Times* newspaper once reported on a drug for treating fear. Certainly, a drug could help with symptoms, but it could never heal the cause! The way out is not moving the deckchairs on the Titanic, but travelling on another ship altogether.

A Course in Miracles would not have us try to make the world better, but instead encourages us to acknowledge the way things are here, accept it and *remember to laugh* at the insanity of the ego's world. (Actually, when you look at it, isn't our near-total slavishness to fear ludicrously funny?)

"All fear is ultimately reducible to the basic misperception that you

have the ability to usurp the power of God" (Text, p. 18) – which is impossible, of course.

By seeing how crazy our world is we get a different perspective. We create a sense of detachment from the illusion and, thus, remember the truth of who we are.

Choosing Again and Again...

"Change your mind."

"Choose again."

This is what *A Course in Miracles* is encouraging us to do whenever we are feeling anything other than the peace of God. But what do these phrases actually mean in a practical sense? They are often bandied about by Course students in an almost glib way. Is it really that easy to "just change your mind about it"? Can it be that changing your mind is just a form of positive thinking, a matter of looking for the "gift" in any situation, or "looking on the 'bright side'"?

It is sometimes said that *A Course in Miracles* is not practical enough. On the contrary, I believe that it is very practical, and we get to practise every day.

"Choosing again" means that we choose a different teacher: the Holy Spirit rather than the ego. We do not have to *do* anything, to struggle to find a new way of looking on our own. All we have to do is to hand over our perceptions to the Holy Spirit. It is that simple. Simple, maybe, but not easy.

I like to think of the ego as being our 'default' option. Unless we have consciously chosen otherwise, we have always already chosen the ego, and not just at times when we are conscious of negative feelings. But it may be easier to recognise our default thinking when we are unhappy, fearful or angry. We would not be experiencing ourselves as being here, in the world, unless we had already made the choice for the ego. It's necessary to realise that choosing the ego does not work, that it brings only pain and unhappiness. We must reach that point before we can choose again and ask for a different teacher.

Our role is simply this:

1. to recognise that the ego's way does not work, that it

brings us pain;
2. to remember that another way is available; and
3. to choose the Holy Spirit as that better way.

The truth that there is nothing to forgive – that there is not even an ego at all – is something that is difficult, if not impossible, for us to realise through any kind of rational thinking. It can only be known through experience. It requires an active agent *outside* our current default thought system to reveal that truth to us.

We choose the Holy Spirit. We do *nothing* else ourselves, other than remember His presence in our minds and choose Him to be our guide instead of the ego. Then the Holy Spirit becomes the active agent, correcting our thinking, showing us a different way. This is an *undoing* of the ego thought system, rather than something we have to *do*.

The Holy Spirit will show us a different way of seeing the situation. His vision will be shown to us if we allow Him to do so. We cannot force it, or make ourselves see things His way, by any kind of wishful thinking or positive affirmation. It will be there only if we choose Him.

If we still find that we feel the same way it is not because the Course doesn't work, the Holy Spirit wasn't listening, or we are so bad as to be beyond redemption. It is because, in truth, we did not want to let the ego go. We wanted to be right, rather than happy. And that is okay. (Notice how the ego will then try to make us feel guilty for *that!*)

It is more powerful and truthful to acknowledge that we do not want to be at peace at any given moment – if lack of peace is our experience in that moment – rather than stubbornly insisting that we do. If we did want peace then we would have it. That's the way it works.

Be honest about negative feelings and do not try to stuff them away in an attempt to be spiritual. It is so easy to misuse the principles of *A Course in Miracles* for denial, to say: "This issue is just an illusion" and to use that as a means to deny that your ego has got you hooked into something. By acknowledging what we are feeling, at least we are being truthful about our starting point. When we want to give up being right, then we will be ready to move on.

The change of mind that ACIM urges is simply the willingness to relinquish the desire to be right, to acknowledge that the default option does not work and that there is a better way. A change in perception will then be *given* to you.

How do you know when you have experienced a miracle? When you feel an overwhelming sense of peace and joy for no apparent reason; when you feel that peace and joy even though nothing "out there" in the world has changed in any way from the way it was before the miracle occurred. Then you know that you have truly let go and asked for vision to be shown to you.

... the Holy Spirit is the Answer to all problems you have made. These problems are not real, but that is meaningless to those who believe in them. And everyone believes in what he made... Into this strange and paradoxical situation... God has sent His Judgment to answer yours. Gently His Judgment substitutes for yours. And through this substitution is the un-understandable made understandable. How is peace possible in this world? In your judgment it is not possible, and can never be possible. But in the Judgment of God what is reflected here is only peace.
(Manual, p. 29)

Giving Ourselves Love

A couple of years ago, I saw a West End musical in which a friend of mine was performing. It was a foot-stompingly great show. The cast seemed to be enjoying themselves hugely and the audience responded with enthusiasm and standing ovations.

Afterwards, I called my friend to congratulate him on his performance. I told him that we loved the fact that the cast was having so much fun. He said that they had felt lifted by the audience's energy.

It struck me that the dynamic in the theatre was a two-way process of giving and receiving. As much as the cast gave, they got back from the audience and vice versa.

A Course in Miracles tells us that this is how it always works. If we withhold from others, we feel diminished. If we withhold appreciation, gratitude, love and forgiveness, we lose. If we cling to what we think we need to keep to ourselves, we are actually ripping ourselves off.

"Never forget you give but to yourself." (Workbook, p. 354) When we extend ourselves in giving, everyone benefits and we give *ourselves* a gift. We feel expansive, powerful, abundant, full and whole. We feel love.

This is a reflection, here on earth, of our true nature, as God knows it. Love can only extend itself. Otherwise, it is not love.

The shining in your mind reminds the world of what it has forgotten, and the world restores the memory to you as well. From you salvation radiates with gifts beyond all measure, given and returned. To you, the giver of the gift, does God Himself give thanks. And in His blessing does the light in you shine brighter, adding to the gifts you have to offer to the world.
(Workbook, p. 357)

When we give in order to get, we are affirming lack and need. This is not giving at all, in the real sense. And we are diminished by reinforcing scarcity. *"When you give ideas away, you strengthen them in your own mind."* (Workbook, p. 354)

I once noticed my own thinking about a friend who was about to achieve success. I thought that if he succeeded, it would mean that I had failed. And if he failed that would, somehow, make me feel better about myself. This is what the ego would have us believe. This is the thinking of the world.

I soon realised that withholding good wishes from my friend meant that I would lose out and feel smaller. I changed my mind, knowing that both of us would be blessed by me expressing my love, rather than my fear. And so would the world.

Give gladly. You can only gain thereby. The thought remains, and grows in strength as it is reinforced by giving.
(Workbook, p. 354)

Let us practise giving freely and generously. That does not mean giving all your money and possessions away; it means giving all your love away. Let us do that and see how rich we feel.

Now are we blessed, and now we bless the world. What we have looked upon we would extend, for we would see it everywhere. We would behold it shining with the grace of God in everyone. We would not have it be withheld from anything we look upon. And to ensure this holy sight is ours, we offer it to everything we see. For where we see it, it will be returned to us in form of lilies we can lay upon our altar, making it a home for Innocence Itself.
(Workbook, pp. 355–6)

When we allow ourselves to express, here, what is true in Heaven, we step closer to awakening to our true nature and to

God. There is no other place to go and no other way to get there. Our only choice is the time we choose to make it so. How about now?

God Is Not Here

Where is God? Good question. According to *A Course in Miracles*, God is not here, in the world. In its view, God did not create the physical universe, the universe of time and space. This may come as a shock to many, but the Course says that in this physical realm, there is nothing that is of God.

Realising that everything here grows old, dies, decays, disintegrates or breaks down has helped me to accept this difficult concept. Obviously our bodies do; but so does everything we make; so does every aspect of nature; and so does the planet itself; even the stars and galaxies – everything. God, being infinite, eternal, unchanging and all-loving, would not and *could* not create anything unlike Himself. Nothing in the physical universe, as we have seen, shares the properties of God. Therefore, God did not create our bodies, nature, the planet, or the physical universe.

The realm of God is also the realm of unity, union, oneness. This physical world is definitely not. In the world there are me and you, us and them, here and there, now and then, good and bad, right and wrong, love and hate. This is a world of differences, of opposites and of separation. This world, as we perceive it, and everything about it, is dualistic and cannot therefore be of God.

So whether we find the idea comfortable or downright objectionable, the Course teaches that God is not here.

We can say that, at best, what we experience in nature, in great works of art, or in our limited experiences of love, are all what the Course calls "echoes of God" – vestiges of remembrance, a ringing through the universe of what lies beyond the universe. Wonderful as these experiences are, any echo is merely a shadow of the real thing. The echo of God is not God himself.

I think the preoccupation with the idea of God being or acting "out there" in the world is really a diversionary tactic. It keeps us from looking to where God really is, inside of us. God is in our minds. We will but to remember Him, but have forgotten where that memory lies.

We are afraid to accept the idea that God is not here, with us in the world, because it seems that we will be accepting our aloneness. What we forget is that we are not where we think we are in the first place. We are not actually here in the world at all; this is a collective hallucination.

The Course is unusual but not unique among spiritual paths in offering the idea that God did not create the world. But it is unconventionally clear on a central point: God did not create us in the form we see – our bodies. Instead, the body is defined as the very symbol of separation. God would no more make bodies than He would make our dream world for us. In fact, the Course says that He doesn't even know about our dream. Dreams are not real; they are not really happening. God does not endow our madness with any degree of legitimacy by recognising its existence.

The good news in all this is that we are *not* alone in separate bodies. Yes, in the world we seem to be alone with our dreams, but in fact we are not in this world. We are where we have always been: safe at Home, with our Creator, in One Love with Him always. We are merely dreaming we are far from Home and don't know that we are dreaming.

> *Do you like what you have made? – a world of murder and attack, through which you thread your timid way through constant dangers, alone and frightened, hoping at most that death will wait a little longer before it overtakes you and you disappear. You made this up. It is a picture of what you think you are; of how you see yourself... The world you see is but a judgment on yourself. It is not there at all.*
> (Text, pp. 429–30)

Competition and Comparison

One of the features of the mistaken belief that we have separated from God is the idea of comparison and, with it, competition. In wanting to be independent of our Source, we also wanted to be number one and better than our brothers. In short, we wanted to be special.

Competition and comparison have always been a feature of my particular ego. First, there was my biological brother, two-and-a-half years younger than I. In my child mind, he usurped my place in the family. My ego told me I had to compete with him for my rightful place and for our parents' love. Quite soon, however, I gave up, believing that I had lost the contest. I pretended I did not care, but I was secretly resentful of the apparent winner, believing that I was less than him.

Over the years, I have worked on this issue and no longer feel the same towards my brother. I have found, however, that the pattern has shifted on to others, usually close friends.

Once a situation occurred in which my competitive tendency was triggered by a friend. I believed he was so much better than me and so much more successful, particularly in the area of relationships (echoing my brother's relationship with our parents). By comparison, I believed that I was not good enough, less than and a failure. Consequently, I was unworthy of all the good things in life.

For a while, I believed this ego-voice was telling the truth. Then I became aware that the ego was no friend of mine. It pretended that it was on my side while actually wanting to grind me into dust with its relentless criticism. Ultimately, it wanted to kill me! Why on earth, then, would I listen to it?

> ... *the ego does not love you. It is unaware of what you are, and wholly mistrustful of everything it perceives...* [It] *is therefore ca-*

pable of suspiciousness at best, viciousness at worst.
(Text, p. 176)

With this realisation came a new clarity of purpose. Within my head, I told the voice clearly to shut the f*** up. And, for a moment, it was quiet. In the resultant space of quiet, I became aware of another voice, the Holy Spirit, singing a different song and telling me the truth.

In the momentary silence of that holy instant, I heard that I am innocent, that I am perfect just the way I am, that there are so many positive and wonderful God-given aspects of my life to be grateful for. Above all, the message was that I am loved and worthy – not because of anything I have done to deserve it, but simply because that is the truth.

... if the Holy Spirit looks with love on all He perceives, He looks with love on you. His evaluation of you is based on His knowledge of what you are, and so He evaluates you truly. And this evaluation must be in your mind, because He is.
(Text, p. 175)

My experience has been, then, that these two voices, the ego and the Holy Spirit, are speaking to me all the time, without pause.

The two voices speak for different interpretations of the same thing simultaneously; or almost simultaneously, for the ego always speaks first.
(Text, pp. 86–7)

I can simply choose which voice I listen to. Whenever the choice is made, it's as if the other voice is temporarily silenced and I fully believe the one to which I am listening. There is no situation in which this choice is not available to all of us.

In the competitive predicament with my friend, having seen

clearly that my ego is not my ally, it was not difficult to choose. Having chosen, the Holy Spirit's voice became undeniable and real. And the relationship was soon transformed by my choice.

My practice now, as soon as I notice that I have chosen wrongly, is simply to listen and choose again.

In every difficulty, all distress, and each perplexity Christ calls to you and gently says, "My brother, choose again."
(Text, p. 666)

The Game of Separateness

The first time I took the Eurostar train through the Channel Tunnel was on a trip from London to Brussels. It took a mere twenty minutes from one end of the tunnel to the other, non-stop from the coast of England to the coast of France – without even getting our feet wet. As a result, I did not think I would ever feel quite the same way again about Britain being an isolated island nation, separated from our continental brothers.

In the same way, I've realised that, having embarked on a spiritual path and experienced a spiritual connection with other people, I can never feel like an 'isolated island', separated from my brothers by the walls our bodies appear to create. Even in my worst moments, the memory of connection is never completely lost. Once we have felt even the slightest hint of the Oneness that lies beyond physical appearances, how can we ever completely forget that we are not separate?

Most of the time, however, we do live behind our seemingly protective walls. Despite the way things look, *A Course in Miracles* says that the separation is not real, that we are not separate from each other or from God. Why, then, does it seem as if we are?

Here is a likely explanation: God, being love, extended Himself to create His one Son, Who is what we collectively are. Then in one crazy moment the Son of God wondered if He might be separate, and forgetting to laugh at such a thought, took the idea seriously. Since His thoughts, like God's, are absolutely creative, suddenly this separated state *was* his reality. At every moment, it is the continuation of that belief in separation that keeps the whole illusion in place.

This was the origin of the body. What could better prove separation than the "realness" of the body? "I *appear* to be a body, and there are others who I can see are separate bodies, so therefore I *must* be one too."

But, the separation is *not* real. Per the logic of the Course, it cannot have happened. If God exists and we are His Son, we cannot be separate, just as a sunbeam cannot be separate from the sun! The Creator and the created cannot be separate.

> *First, you believe that what God created can be changed by your own mind. Second, you believe that what is perfect can be rendered imperfect or lacking. Third, you believe that you can distort the creations of God, including yourself... These related distortions represent a picture of what actually occurred in the separation, or the "detour into fear." None of this existed before the separation, nor does it actually exist now.*
> (Text, p. 17)

When observing people in conflict, I increasingly hear a voice in my head saying, "They are just egos who believe they are separate." I can laugh about them fighting over their little piece of turf, defending their bodies, or fighting over whose body is with whom. "Oh, I get it. They think they *are* those bodies!" I am beginning to see the joke, the ridiculous idea. Perhaps the Son of God is beginning to laugh again!

What I have to do, though, is constantly remind myself that I, too, am not a body. It is not always easy. I know, however, that forgiveness heals the perception of separation.

It was *belief* in the reality of the separation that started the whole thing going, and I suppose it will be the last belief to be dispelled before the Atonement returns us to the state we never left.

> *Salvation must reverse the mad belief in separate thoughts and separate bodies, which lead separate lives and go their separate ways.*
> (Workbook, p. 180)

The Thought Police

Beware of the spiritual Gestapo, or thought police, particularly of the *A Course in Miracles* variety – whether they take the form of fellow students on the path or the voice in your own head!

You know the kind of situation. You get sick, for example. Or you are late, you don't stick to the agreed plan, you get rather merrier at the Christmas party than is deemed appropriate, or you indulge in a special relationship or in fear-based or unspiritual thinking… you name a human weakness and they will get you for it! Rather than practise what the Course says – that is, forgiveness – the spiritual Gestapo, believing that the role of a good Course student is to police the universe, will judge you, tell you how you are falling short, or inform you that you're are an out-and-out failure. This may be dressed up as saving you from yourself but, really, it is judgement and attack.

It is no wonder that Ken Wapnick talked about being wary of some apparently well-meaning Course students. In particular, I think it is the new converts and zealots who see the errors in everyone else's ways – and thus miss the point entirely.

Worse still, by far, are the *inner* thought police, who will condemn us more thoroughly and brutally than any external critic. The raucous shrieking in our own minds can be deafening at times.

The Course is well aware and accepting of our humanness and does not expect or demand purity. In the context of preparing the ground for the holy instant and being in full communication with Spirit, it simply says:

> *The necessary condition for the holy instant does not require that you have no thoughts that are not pure. But it does require that you have none that you would keep.*

(Text, p. 311)

The ego, being our greatest enemy, will insist that those impure thoughts are proof that we are bad, worthless, unlovable or downright evil. Instead, the Course merely reminds us that it is not in our best interests to hang on to such thoughts.

With guilt featuring so prominently in the ego's arsenal of weapons against us, we may then feel bad for feeling bad, judge ourselves for having judgements and feel guilty for having guilty thoughts. This is the double bind I have written about before – one more turn of the screw by the ego in torturing ourselves in order to keep us stuck in guilt. Rather than buying into that guilt, it is much healthier to laugh at the ego and say: "There it is again! Judging me for being a mere human. So, what's new?" It is okay to be human and have human foibles!

Nothing we can do as mere humans can possibly alter or diminish our God-created innocence, however hard we may try and however harshly the world may judge us. All we have done is to make the error of forgetting our innocence, and all we need to do is to stop listening to the thought police and remember the Truth – by forgiving ourselves and others.

Chapter 15 goes on to say that: *"Innocence is not of your making. It is given you the instant you would have it."* (Text, p. 311)

My favourite lesson, Lesson 131, says:

Remember often that today should be a time of special gladness, and refrain from dismal thoughts and meaningless laments. Salvation's time has come. Today is set by Heaven itself to be a time of grace for you and for the world. If you forget this happy fact, remind yourself with this: "Today I seek and find all that I want. My single purpose offers it to me. No one can fail who seeks to reach the truth." (Workbook, p. 241)

The Moment of Bliss

Over the years, I have lost count of newcomers to *A Course in Miracles* who have spoken to me, full of enthusiasm and excitement, about finding "this wonderful Course". Their conversation goes something like: "Wow, I'm so happy that I found this book. My life is full of joy, miracles and amazing things happening."

While I am careful to reflect this enthusiasm back to them and feel it would be unkind to dampen it in any way, I also know that, in most cases, what they are experiencing is not the real transformation we are promised by the Course. How could it be, in just a month or two? How could they find the experience of doing a course that *"aims at a complete reversal of thought"* (Manual, p. 60) so easy? Would not such a complete reversal be difficult, challenging, uncomfortable and probably painful?

I remember going through my own Bliss Stage early on. It seemed, since discovering the Course, that all my problems had been solved and my life was going to be continuously joyful from that point on. But I wasn't really 'getting it'.

Some years later, I spent a week at Ken Wapnick's retreat centre in Roscoe, New York (now located in Temecula, California) to attend a workshop on "The Obstacles to Peace". Listening to Ken's discourse on the final obstacle, the Fear of God, I was overcome with fear at the sudden realisation that if I was going to go the distance and finally awaken, it would mean that everything I thought of myself as being, everything I thought I knew, had to 'die'. The present 'I' would be no more; my body, individuality and personality would cease to be and I would "disappear into God". This felt like death because it would be the death of the ego. I could not believe that the spiritual path I had happily followed thus far was leading to the inevitable end of *me*! I was in panic.

Later that day, at lunchtime, Ken was coming down the lunch queue chatting to everyone. When he reached me, I told him that I was in total terror after the morning session. "That's good," he remarked.

"How can this be good?" I asked.

"Because you are no longer in denial," he replied. And he was right.

The ego is happy to be "spiritual" until its foundations are threatened, as they eventually must be, and from that point on it is not going to be a smooth ride.

To learn this course requires willingness to question every [belief] *that you hold. Not one can be kept hidden and obscure but it will jeopardize your learning.*
(Text, p. 499)

Hold on to your hats. It's going to get bumpy!

Empty your mind of everything it thinks is either true or false, or good or bad, of every thought it judges worthy, and all the ideas of which it is ashamed. Hold onto nothing. Do not bring with you one thought the past has taught, nor one belief you ever learned before from anything.
(Workbook, p. 360)

Why we would undertake such a journey to the end of all that the ego holds dear? But, truly, what else is there to do? To *not* do so is to live a lie, a pain-filled life with no hope of respite. What we are offered, if we are willing to let go, is to awaken to a blissful Reality, eternal Truth and infinite Love beyond anything we can imagine in this tiny, separated state of ours. Undoing of the old takes us toward the happy dream and Heaven.

To know that this undoing is probably going to be experienced as painful is to be forewarned, so that we do not think something is wrong when the going gets tough, when enthusiasm can turn to disillusionment. At such times, we can be tempted to think the Course is to blame, or that we are doing it wrong.

> *Under the ego's dark foundation is the memory of God, and it is of this that you are really afraid. For this memory would instantly restore you to your proper place, and it is this place that you have sought to leave... Therefore, you have used the world to cover your love, and the deeper you go into the blackness of the ego's foundation, the closer you come to the Love that is hidden there. And it is this that frightens you.*
> (Text, pp. 242–3)

Are we prepared to recognise this and be okay with it?

Forgiving Myself

Forgiveness as taught by *A Course in Miracles* is a truly radical concept, going far beyond what is normally signified by the word. To the world, forgiveness is a noble but slightly soft option. If we are feeling kind and generous we may let someone whom we feel has wronged us 'off the hook'. In so doing, we might feel that we have somehow done ourselves a disservice or not been strong enough; we might have been truer to ourselves if we'd stood our ground and maintained a righteous indignation.

A Course in Miracles blows this idea out of the water. I remember, years ago, at one of the first Course groups I went to, when the penny suddenly dropped for me. "Oh, I get it!" I exclaimed. "Forgiveness is for *my* benefit."

The Course goes so far as to say that: *"Forgiveness is the key to happiness."* (Workbook, p. 214) Let us be clear. It does not say that forgiveness is one of the keys to happiness; it is *the* key.

Lesson 122 says: *"Forgiveness offers everything I want"* (Workbook, p. 217) – not *many* things I might want but *everything* I want. How radical is that? The lesson begins:

What could you want forgiveness cannot bring? Do you want peace… happiness, a quiet mind, a certainty of purpose… a sense of worth and beauty… care and safety… sure protection always… quietness that cannot be disturbed, a gentleness that never can be hurt… All this forgiveness offers you, and more.

Well, I'm sold!

But just think what other things we often feel are the keys to our happiness: getting well if we are sick; getting richer if we are poor; getting a relationship if we do not have one; getting out of a relationship we do not like; getting an exciting new job to replace our dead-end one; and so on. The list goes on and on and may include changing anything and everything in the outside world, instead of doing the inner work that the Course is advocating. *"Forgiveness is the key to happiness."*

Lesson 121 lists many things that are the result of the unforgiving mind:

> *The unforgiving mind is full of fear, and offers love no room to be itself... is sad, without the hope of respite and release from pain... The unforgiving mind is torn with doubt, confused about itself and all it sees; afraid and angry, weak and blustering, afraid to go ahead, afraid to stay, afraid to waken or go to sleep... The unforgiving mind sees no mistakes, but only sins. It looks upon the world with sightless eyes, and shrieks as it beholds its own projections rising to attack its miserable parody of life... The unforgiving mind is in despair, without the prospect of a future which can offer anything but more despair.*
> (Workbook, p. 214)

When you think of carrying that kind of burden on your shoulders, is there any way you could ever be happy unless you forgive? No way, indeed.

Many of us reach *A Course in Miracles* after trying other paths which did not bring the results they promised, did not satisfy us or bring us happiness. I wonder how many of these paths made forgiveness the key! Many of us have tried New Age teachings and philosophies. We've believed that if we try the healing power of light, crystals, soul therapy, angels, or chi energy, etc, then one of those magical elements will bring us happiness.

I am not saying that there is anything wrong with any of these things or that they are not beneficial in some way, but can they offer what the Course tells us that forgiveness offers? We would rather try anything than remember that *"Forgiveness is the key to happiness."* (Workbook, p. 214)

People often ask my advice about problems they are facing

with people and situations in their lives, and the pain it is causing them. I have realised that the answer to all these problems is very simple, but is often the last thing people consider. When I suggest giving up analysing, negotiating, changing behaviour patterns or filing lawsuits, and instead to try forgiveness, the response usually is: "Oh, I didn't think of that."

"Forgiveness is the key to happiness" because forgiveness of others, yourself and circumstances returns your awareness to the truth. It releases your mind from the misperception of sin, guilt and punishment that is burdening your mind. It releases you from resentment, at the same time as it releases others from the accusation of guilt. It can do that because the belief in sin is now seen to be a mistake. Then, attack can be seen to do no real harm, because what is real in you cannot be harmed in any way. Thus any attack is seen as the call for love that it truly is. *"Forgiveness is the key to happiness"* because our ultimate source of happiness, our eternal, unbroken Union with God, is now experienced as being a living, breathing reality – if only momentarily.

The Inner Sat Nav

Do you have a Sat Nav (GPS)? I love mine. I only recently bought one, having held out because I didn't think I needed one. I had always managed without and had never got into serious difficulty. But, if I am honest, I had got lost a few times and had often taken longer to reach my destination than I needed to.

I am now a convert. With my Sat Nav, I can relax, knowing that it knows the way. I have a more relaxed and peaceful journey. Its sole purpose is to lead me to my destination or to guide me home. I can afford to trust it because it has the bigger picture. It knows about road conditions and traffic hold-ups of which I am unaware, and thus can recalculate to derive an alternative route that saves me from getting trapped or delayed.

All this is available to me if I choose to listen and take notice. Sometimes, though, I think I know better. "No, surely, that can't be the best way" I say in response to the Sat Nav's guidance. Deciding I know a preferable route, I take it, and invariably get held up at roadworks or take longer to reach my destination than I thought.

If I can accept that my Sat Nav knows better than I do and trust it to guide me, I am often surprised by how easy a journey is, or how quickly I get there.

Equally reassuring is the knowledge that at each step of the way, if I've decided to devise my own route, I can change my mind and choose to listen to the available guidance instead. My Sat Nav is constantly recalculating the most direct route from any given point. If I make a mistake and take a wrong turn, it instantly knows, and will guide me back to the correct route without saying, "How stupid you were!"

I have realised, of course, that my Sat Nav experience is analogous to my experience with the Holy Spirit, my inner Guide. The Holy Spirit knows the way home and I do not.

I will not use my own past learning as the light to guide me now. By this refusal to attempt to teach yourself what you do not know, the Guide Whom God has given you will speak to you.
(Text, p. 298)

Guiding you to the Home you never left is the Holy Spirit's job.

His is the Voice that calls you back to where you were before and will be again. It is possible even in this world to hear only that Voice and no other.
(Text, p. 75)

The Holy Spirit is able to see the whole picture and make allowances for factors of which I am unaware. *"The Holy Spirit is the Christ Mind which is aware of the knowledge that lies beyond perception."* (Text, p. 74) This Voice is available all the time, but does not control or force me. *"God's Voice speaks to me all through the day."* (Workbook, p. 78)

The Voice of the Holy Spirit does not command, because It is incapable of arrogance. It does not demand, because It does not seek control. It does not overcome, because It does not attack. It merely reminds... It brings to your mind the other way, remaining quiet even in the midst of the turmoil you may make.
(Text, p. 76)

I can choose to listen to this *"still small voice"* (Text, p. 456) and follow, or not.

Today He speaks to you. His Voice awaits your silence, for His Word cannot be heard until your mind is quiet for a while, and meaningless desires have been stilled. Await His Word in quiet.
(Workbook, p. 225)

When I do not listen I invariably become stuck. When I listen, I am able to relax and be at peace. I am guided quickly to the perfect outcome even though I often question the route. If I go off course, I am corrected. It is a beautiful experience.

> ... *where you made a faulty choice before you now can make a better one, and thus escape all pain that what you chose before has brought to you.*
> (Text, p. 666)

> *A healed mind... carries out the plans that it receives through listening to wisdom that is not its own. It waits until it has been taught what should be done, and then proceeds to do it.*
> (Workbook, p. 253)

I thoroughly recommend listening to your internal Sat Nav. Have a good journey. Bon voyage!

The World is a Mirror

Don't you just love the idea that the world reflects back to you what is going on in your own mind? It says that our worst enemy, our favourite hate figure (and don't we all have them?) is merely a reflection of our own dark thoughts. Is this not an idea that we relish? Aren't we grateful to the Course for telling us that?

No; not a bit of it! This concept can bring up our greatest resistance.

And isn't that the nub of the matter? We don't want to look at the darkness within our ego minds, preferring to project it on to others. "No, it's not me; it's them!" At this very moment, you might even be making me a hate figure, if you don't like what I am writing!

If we can acknowledge our resistance to this idea, then we have caught ourselves in the very act that our resistance was designed to obscure. The Course says that this whole world is a defence against the truth, against God. Our preoccupation with what is going on outside ourselves, in the world, keeps us from looking at the place where it is really all happening – in our minds.

According to the Course, we all feel guilty about our self-imposed separation from God, although we are not usually consciously aware of it. Instead, we attempt to get rid of our pain and guilt, firstly by denying that we feel it, and secondly, in an attempt to make sure it is not really there, by projecting it outside ourselves on to others. By doing this, we believe that we have disposed of the guilt inside us and feel instantly relieved, if only temporarily. The other person is now the focus of our displeasure, or even our outright hatred.

We think that it is our spouse, partner, parent, boss, neighbour, or government who is making us feel unhappy, and that they are the cause of all our problems. If only they would be different, then we would be happy! We think: "If I make someone else guilty and responsible for me feeling this way, then I will be innocent. Thus I am better and more righteous than these others." And: "I will be okay because so-and-so is not."

The problem with projection is that it does not work. It only serves to increase the feelings of guilt and pain, which we are trying to reduce. Because we cannot condemn one part of the Sonship without condemning all of it, we cannot condemn another without condemning ourselves.

> *... projection will always hurt you... It is solely a device of the ego to make you feel different from your brothers and separated from them. The ego justifies this on the grounds that it makes you seem 'better' than they are, thus obscuring your equality with them still further... The ego uses projection only to destroy your perception of both yourself and your brothers.*
> (Text, p. 96)

The only way out is to take back our projections through forgiveness. In that way, we will see the whole facade dissolve in front of us. If we can see the other person as innocent, then we will see ourselves as innocent. If we extend love to them, we love ourselves. A lose-lose situation can become a win-win. Without sin, we finally see ourselves and one another as we truly are: the children of a loving Father, created perfectly in His image.

> *When you meet anyone, remember it is a holy encounter. As you see him you will see yourself. As you treat him you will treat yourself. As you think of him you will think of yourself. Never forget this, for in him you will find yourself or lose yourself. Whenever two Sons of God meet, they are given another chance at salvation. Do not leave anyone without giving salvation to him and receiving it yourself.*
> (Text, p. 142)

We can start to unravel the apparently complex web of our lives by taking back our projections. We can begin to make sense of this mysterious "life-thing we do" (as we jokingly referred to it at a study group I once attended). Not that we actually need to understand it all; with forgiveness literally undoing the effects of the past, we could give up our therapists and analysts, and stop trying to figure it all out.

Life really can become our 'magic mirror' telling us all we need to know about the beliefs we hold about ourselves in our subconscious minds. To use the film projector and screen analogy, if we don't like the film, it is no good going up to the screen to fix it. We have to return to the projector to change the film. Or as the Course puts it, "... *seek not to change the world, but choose to change your mind about the world.*" (Text, p. 445)

About *A Course in Miracles*

A Course in Miracles (ACIM) is a self-study system of spiritual psychology contained in a 1250-page, three-volume book, which was first published in 1976. The Course contains a synthesis of the teachings that lie at the core of the world's great religions, together with sophisticated psychological insight. It emphasises the practical application of its principles, which focus on forgiveness and, thus, the transformational potential of the mind. It has touched the lives of millions of people around the world.

The Course teaches that there is no separation between God and ourselves or, therefore, between us. God is love, eternal and infinite, and all there is. We are God's one creation. God only creates like Himself, so we remain as God created us, innocent and whole. Only what God created is real. God did not create pain, death, guilt or fear, so although they exist in our experience, they are not real. The Course aims at removing the blocks to the awareness of love's presence. Rather than trying to change external circumstances, the Course teaches us to change our perceptions about the world. The peace of God is reached through the practice of forgiveness.

This is a course in miracles. It is a required course. Only the time you take it is voluntary. Free will does not mean that you can establish the curriculum. It means only that you can elect what you want to take at a given time. The course does not aim at teaching the meaning of love, for that is beyond what can be taught. It does aim, however, at removing the blocks to the awareness of love's presence, which is your natural inheritance. The opposite of love is fear, but what is all-encompassing can have no opposite. This course can therefore be summed up very simply in this way:

"Nothing real can be threatened. Nothing unreal exists. Herein

lies the peace of God."
(From Introduction to the Text)

About Miracle Network

The Miracle Network is a UK-Registered Charity (reg. number 1108852), acting as a resource organisation for all things related to *A Course in Miracles* in the UK. Its website is http://www.miracles.org.uk/

The Miracle Network:

- offers free support, contact and information service for 3,500 students of *A Course in Miracles*, mainly in the United Kingdom, although the Network also has members overseas.
- publishes a bimonthly magazine, *Miracle Worker*, which contains news, thought-provoking and inspiring articles, an events guide (Course-related events all over the UK) and listings of ACIM study and support groups.
- organises its own Course-related talks, workshops and classes, at both local and national level, as well as a biannual conference. The *Miracle Cafe* runs on the last Thursday evening of every month in London.
- provides a mail-order service for the lowest UK prices on all Course-related books, CDs and computer programs. Many of these items are difficult or impossible to obtain in ordinary bookshops in the UK. See the website for the list of publications available.
- maintains a list of ACIM Support Groups nationwide, which is printed in every issue of *Miracle Worker*. Many students have found that joining a study group has contributed greatly to their understanding of the Course, and has given them new friends and support. For the most up-to-date list see the website.

These services are provided on a voluntary basis, so the Miracle

Network welcomes new UK subscribers to *Miracle Worker* magazine and gratefully accepts additional donations to cover our costs and to cover those currently unable to pay.

For details and access to all of the above, visit http://www.miracles.org.uk.

About Ian Patrick

Ian Patrick worked as a geologist in the oil industry for nearly 20 years. He has been a student/teacher of *A Course in Miracles* since 1991. An inspiration to many, he founded the Miracle Network and began writing insightful articles for its magazine *Miracle Worker* in 1994, and is currently the charity's Manager/ Coordinator. He has spoken about the Course on radio, TV and at international conferences. He has been facilitating ACIM workshops internationally since 1998 and teaches from knowledge and experience with incisiveness, clarity, vision and humour.

He says: "I was turned off religion as a child. I didn't 'get' it and, somehow, I felt the message of Christianity was 'not quite right'. As a very young child, I had some very profound ideas about life, God and the nature of existence – things I heard nowhere else (until I found *A Course in Miracles*) but, nevertheless, felt were true.

"Studying geology at school and university, I gradually forgot about this and adopted a more deterministic view of life. If you had asked me in my 20s about God, I would have said that I was an atheist. I was 'successful', with a career in the oil industry, money, property, opportunities to travel and an active social life, but I still felt something was missing. My life seemed rather pointless, directionless, flat and empty. At one point, I was expressing this dissatisfaction to a friend and he told me about 'a course' someone had recommended. I knew nothing about it, but was desperate enough to sign up. Some people I met there, eventually, led me to *A Course in Miracles*.

"The Course was a coming home for me. Once I discovered that the Course's Christian terminology had psychological, rather than religious, meaning, I had one of many 'light bulb' moments. It brought a recognition of what, deep down, I always knew to be true and brought new purpose, meaning and perspective to my life. It is not that life is necessarily always easy now, but it is better – or, perhaps, it is not that it is better now, but it is easier! Whatever happens, whatever challenges I appear to face, there is a context for it, which is profoundly reassuring. My life is richer and my experience deeper. My relationships are easier, more fulfilling and intimate. I know that I am on a path, a journey without distance to a goal that has never changed.

"I felt I was 'led' to set up the Miracle Network and to it becoming my full-time job. Certainly, it was never my conscious choice. I always, simply, took the next step and that is where I ended up!! Since the Course has become my work, I cannot escape so easily into old, ego patterns. I am being constantly reminded of the principles and that I have another choice. I know that there is no going back now, that I will continue my work and that I will complete the curriculum and reach the goal the Course promises.

"I think the greatest single gift the Course has brought me is an understanding and an experience of what true forgiveness is and how forgiveness not only helps transform difficult situations and relationships, but how it actually heals my own mind of its guilt, negative beliefs and negative self-concepts. Forgiveness truly is the Course's tool and, therefore, my tool for transformation. I cannot, now, imagine life without this or without *A Course in Miracles*."

Acknowledgements

I would like to extend my eternal gratitude to the following people for helping to make this book possible: Robert Holden, without whose inspiration and encouragement I may never have started writing and teaching about *A Course in Miracles*; D. Patrick Miller for his publishing expertise and editing skills for the original, Fearless Books edition of this book; Jon Mundy for writing the Foreword; Nick Williams for his guidance and prodding; Nouk Sanchez for supporting my work; Philip Bradbury for most of the section titles; Diane Cross for her early proofreading; and Kamlan Munsamy for his cover photography. https://www.behance.net/kamlanmcd4a

Special mentions need to be given to: Jeremy Walters for his friendship and encouragement; Marianne Duggan; Annie Neville; Nick Davis; Alison Atwell for always being there at the major turning points of my spiritual life; and my family for their love and for inadvertently providing me with my life lessons, which form some of the material for this book.

My thanks are also due to every one of the many people who have helped in innumerable ways with running the Miracle Network since 1994. You are too numerous to mention, individually, but you know who you are.

I also want to thank all the wonderful *A Course in Miracles* teachers, from whom I have learned so much over the years and to mention some significant ones: Marianne Williamson, the late Kenneth Wapnick, Tom Carpenter, the late Michael Portelley, Chuck Spezzano, Duane O'Kane, Jerry and Lee Jampolsky, Michael Dawson, Robert Perry and others.

Finally, this book would not exist without *A Course in Miracles* itself, so my profound appreciation goes to the 'author' and to those who brought the Course into the world.

BOOKS

O is a symbol of the world, of oneness and unity. In different cultures it also means the "eye," symbolizing knowledge and insight. We aim to publish books that are accessible, constructive and that challenge accepted opinion, both that of academia and the "moral majority."

Our books are available in all good English language bookstores worldwide. If you don't see the book on the shelves ask the bookstore to order it for you, quoting the ISBN number and title. Alternatively you can order online (all major online retail sites carry our titles) or contact the distributor in the relevant country, listed on the copyright page.

See our website www.o-books.com for a full list of over 500 titles, growing by 100 a year.

And tune in to myspiritradio.com for our book review radio show, hosted by June-Elleni Laine, where you can listen to the authors discussing their books.